Paul Mendelson is the London *Financial Times* bridge correspondent, and a leading author on bridge, poker and casino gambling.

Paul switched from chess to bridge while still at school, and has stayed with the game. Although competitive, he only rarely plays tournament bridge these days, but he can claim The National Schools' Championship (a while back now), representing England in the European Friendly Games in 1984, two gold and two silver medals in several Mind Sports Olympiads and The Scottish National Championships – pairs and teams trophies, as well as numerous county and regional events.

Paul is the author of six books on bridge, three books on poker, and a huge book on the statistically correct way to play every casino game. He writes the *Financial Times*' bridge column weekly and his articles appear in magazines throughout the world. For many years the administrator of The Macallan International Pairs Championship, Paul is known to many of the world's finest players and is constantly seeking high-level innovations for his teaching and play.

His interactive lectures are renowned, allowing players of all standards to improve their game. Never relying on rules, he insists on explaining the logical thought processes behind each decision. His students have gone on to win many competitions, and he has coached expert players, training them for international competition.

D1322518

Also by Paul Mendelson

Bridge for Complete Beginners
The Right Way to Play Bridge
Bridge: Winning Ways to Play Your Cards
Texas Hold'em Poker: Begin and Win
Texas Hold'em Poker: Win Online
The Mammouth Book of Poker
The Mammouth Book of Casino Games

The First Rule of Survival
'An excellent uncompromising thriller made even better by its setting ... the story is two journeys in one, and I'm glad I took both.' Lee Child

'A jaw-droppingly brilliant crime thriller. Imagine *The Killing* moved to Cape Town and into a landscape of the hot and dusty African veld.' Philip Glenister

THE GOLDEN RULES
of Bridge

Paul Mendelson

Constable & Robinson Ltd.
55–56 Russell Square
London WC1B 4HP
www.constablerobinson.com

First published in the UK by How To Books,
an imprint of Constable & Robinson Ltd., 2014

A copy of the British Library Cataloguing in
Publication Data is available from the British Library

ISBN: 978-0-71602-359-3 (paperback)
ISBN: 978-1-8452-8553-1 (ebook)

Printed and bound in the UK

1 3 5 7 9 10 8 6 4 2

CONTENTS

INTRODUCTION

THERE ARE NO RULES.

That's it. That's the first sentence of a book called *The Golden Rules of Bridge*.

The point, however, is that many players – and most students – seem to think that bridge is about remembering what to do. It isn't. It is, as I tell my students – especially the men – a thinking woman's game. To play well, you have to work out what to do, based on the guiding principles of the game, your knowledge of your opponents, and your own gut feelings. As you improve, there may be probabilities to consider, and combinations of plays. Reading a flipper or remembering a parrot-fashion-learnt bid won't help you in the real world.

There are guidelines – rules, if you wish – but they are to guide, not to insist that you follow them. When I use the word 'never' that means, 'almost never'; the word 'always', 'almost always'. Bridge is about judgement and understanding. If you do not understand what you are doing, you will never make a good player.

1

However, there are some themes and understandings which, if you have them firmly in mind as you play, will definitely help you to improve, whether you are a social player, a club devotee, or a regular at Duplicate Pairs.

There are ideas which are so powerful that the thought of playing bridge without them seems ridiculous – yet, for years, that's exactly what I did. Partners were quick to criticize but slow to inform. Once you know about the existence of something it is easier to look for it; if you don't know it's there, how can you ever see it? Now, I try to ensure that all my students hear about these principles as soon as they are ready. Once assimilated, I believe that they will help you to think correctly about each problem.

Whilst there are always exceptions, there are certain standard ways in which bridge works. Everything moves clockwise (that's surprisingly important); it's why a six-card suit is so much more powerful than a five-card suit; why if one side holds an eight-card fit, the other side will hold one too; why, if you assume that the leader against a no-trump contract has a five-card suit, this will guide you to the best way to approach the hand; why, in competitive bidding, trump length, not points, becomes the determining factor as to how high you should compete. Once you understand these principles in each of the key areas, not only will you play better, but you will enjoy your game so much more.

The first chapter of this book – 'The Bonfire of the Rules' – is a polemic on the mindlessness of most of the rules created for bridge. It is deliberately acerbic and grumpy, because I witness these so-called rules doing much more harm than good and the world would be a better place without them. I hope that, when you've read through the chapter, you'll see why. However, the real answers come in the following chapters where, I hope, I will succeed in getting you to think about your actions rather than just doing what some textbook, flipper, chart or tweet has told you to do.

Paul Mendelson
London

CHAPTER ONE

THE BONFIRE OF THE RULES

T o FREE YOUR MIND to allow you to think about bridge, you must discard those destructive habits of referring to flippers or summaries, following flow charts or hunting for bridge tip apps. To enjoy bridge to its fullest – and to improve and to continue to improve – you must understand why everything at the bridge table happens. If you learn it by rote, or refer to a table of numbers, you will forever be tied to your crutches and be unable to get up and walk for yourself. So, I say unto ye, throw off your crutches!

I've made it sound like an evangelical sermon because, like so many bad habits, rule obeying is highly addictive. It seems like the answer to all your problems, but it is an illusion. And it is important, because nothing breaks my heart more than seeing someone wondering what to bid, spending their valuable time flipping through a flipper or flowing down a flow chart, only to have no idea why they make the bid they are told to make. If you know why you should bid something, you are much more likely to pick the right suit and the correct level. So, let's spend a couple of moments pulling down these monuments to thoughtlessness.

Burn those rules

To start, the so-called Rule of 20. This mind-numbingly stupid rule states that if you add the number of points to the number of cards in your two longest suits and the total comes to 20, you can open the bidding. This is awful; really mindless. Do the creators of this rule really think these two hands are the same?

(a)	(b)
♠ J6432	♠ KQJ85
♥ AJ	♥ 6
♦ Q7432	♦ KJ1086
♣ Q	♣ 93

According to the Rule of 20, both these hands warrant an opening bid. Being a discerning player yourself, naturally you can see that hand (a) is a dreadful load of old rubbish on which, if you open the bidding, you will simply mislead your partner and assist your opponents. Hand (b), if you are so inclined, is a perfectly decent opening bid where your values are concentrated in your long suits and the playing potential of the hand far outweighs its modest point count. Any rule which plumps these two disparate hands in the same category is clearly bonkers.

The superior principle is to say that an opening bid shows 12 high-card points, unless it contains a six-card suit or longer. This correctly values the power of a six-card suit over a hand containing only a five-card suit, and takes into account all your Weak Twos, Weak Threes, and Acol light opening hands which all good players use. Naturally, if you pick up a splendid, focused collection (with all your high cards in your two long suits and excellent playing potential) as in hand (b), you can choose – as a thinking person – to open that hand and justify your decision with ease to any subsequent questioning.

Incidentally, hands such as hand (b) can often be described best by passing originally and then entering the auction later with an Unusual NT Overcall or Michaels Cue-bid. This gives you time to assess what your opponents might have before committing your side to too high a level.

I think that the modern expert style would be to open with hand (b), however, since bidding first often provides a substantial advantage. By the way, do not enter the auction with an Unusual NT or any other two-suited overcall when your suits are as bad as hand (a) – this will only lead to trouble.

The Rule of 20, or more properly the Rule of 19, was invented to help directors of Duplicate tournaments to decide whether a player's opening bid was legitimate or should be

considered a 'psychic' bid (one designed to mislead the opponents). These rules were never envisaged as a guide to the
player as to when you should open and when you should pass.

So, we've binned the Rule of 20 – and the Rule of 19. Now,
what about the Rules of 3, 5, 7, 11, 14, 18, 23, ad nauseam?
The Rule of 11 has some redeeming features in that it can
inform an otherwise unthinking player that his opponent
perhaps holds only one, maybe two, cards higher than the
one originally led, but the advantages of this rule can just
as easily be worked out by thinking. The Rule of 7 can be
superseded by thinking about your opponent's lead against
no-trumps (see page 153); the Rule of 14, by analysis of
your hand in relation to partner's opening bid (see page
19). The others just don't bear any further contemplation.

Of course, there are understandings that may be considered as rules which are perfectly sensible, like 'open the
higher-ranking of two five-card suits, except with clubs and
spades' – when you should open 1C.

If you stop to think about how the auction will develop,
you will almost certainly make this decision anyway, since
the auction

1S	2D
3C	

is space-wasting, dangerous and should show upwards of
17pts, leaving you to rebid 2S if you have fewer points, and

so hide your second five-card suit altogether; whereas

1C	1D
1S	

is economical, forcing, and leaves plenty of room to show your fifth spade when you make your third bid.

As a basic rule, anything that is called 'The rule of' something is going to be pretty lousy. You see what I did there? I described the dismissing of rules called rules as 'a rule'. And that's how easy it is to slip into this nonsense.

The Losing Trick Count

Many excellent players invoke the Losing Trick Count and it is a fine additional check when you are deciding how high you might support your partner. It is particularly effective when you hold a 4-4 fit, or 5-4 fit, but becomes markedly less accurate as the trump fit varies. For example, if you have 7-1 trump fit, the Losing Trick Count is utterly useless.

I like to utilize it when deciding whether to raise my partner to 2, 3 or 4 of his major suit, and whether or not slam potential exists when I have agreed a suit at a lower level. Used properly, including the essential basic adjustments, the Losing Trick Count is a useful tool indeed. Sadly, I more often hear this:

♠ 2
♥ KQJ76
♦ KQJ54
♣ Q3

'My partner opened 1S and I jumped to 3H, because I only had five losers and that means it's going to be a slam, and I couldn't just bid 2H because partner wouldn't know how strong I was.'

This is, of course, poppycock. This hand doesn't contain five losers, because you haven't yet found a fit, and although your partner has no more idea what you have when you bid 3H than if you had bid 2H, now he just has less bidding space to find out. The correct latter option allows you to develop the auction correctly; the blame-it-on-the-Losing-Trick-Count first option just ruins your own auction.

So, if you would like to play the Losing Trick Count – and I recommend that you do – just remember that no hand is worth assessing for losers until you are about to raise your partner with four-card support, or you have been raised and are wondering how high to go now.

How many losers does this hand contain?

♠ Q6432

♥ 63

♦ AKQ

♣ 853

It certainly does not contain seven losers because you haven't agreed a suit or, indeed, have any idea in which denomination you might play. To justify an opening bid with this by claiming only seven losers is just plain nonsense. This is a jolly fine pass.

Your partner opens 1H and you hold these hands. What do you respond?

(a)	(b)	(c)
♠ 92	♠ 2	♠ 5
♥ K843	♥ Q952	♥ KJ74
♦ 952	♦ KQJ54	♦ 73
♣ AQ98	♣ 963	♣ AKQ843

(a) 3H. This hand is too good for a raise to 2H and, since you have four-card support for your partner's suit, you need only count one (and a bit) loser in the heart suit, leaving you eight losers.

(b) 4H. With seven losers and a weak hand, 4H is worth a punt. Your opponents may well be making 3S or 4S, so even if your partner does not make 4H, it should be the right spot for you. If partner has a five-card heart suit and A♦, 4H may well make.

11

(c) 3C. You may only have 13pts, but your hand is massive now that partner has opened a suit for which you hold four-card support. The Losing Trick Count is an excellent guide as to whether to jump-shift when you have four-card support for your partner. With five losers or less, it will probably work best to jump-shift and develop the auction from here using cue-bids and Roman Key-Card Blackwood (RKCB).

The power of the six-card suit

Having been pretty angry and negative so far, it's time to look at something about which we should rejoice: the six-card suit. You may have noticed that six-card suits are usually required for opening at the 2-level, whether strong or weak, and the reason for this is that with a six-card suit the chances of you holding an eight-card fit with your partner are very high, whereas with only a five-card suit, the chances are against you and your partner holding an eight-card fit.

Think of it like this: if you have six cards, there are seven other cards in the suit. Divided between three players, on average each player will hold $2\frac{1}{3}$ cards in that suit, giving you a nice $8\frac{1}{3}$-card fit (or, what we like to call: an eight-card fit).

Whereas, holding only a five-card suit, the other players share eight cards and have, on average, $2\frac{2}{3}$ cards, giving you less than an eight-card fit.

This is also why bidding a pre-empt at the 3-level with

a seven-card suit is sound, since with six cards out, each player is likely to hold two cards, giving you a nine-card fit.

This is why, for me, these two hands are so different:

(a)	(b)
♠ J6432	♠ KQJ852
♥ AJ	♥ 6
♦ 43	♦ KJ8
♣ KQ86	♣ 932

Hand (a) is not an opening hand for many reasons, the main one being that, if you open 1S, what will you rebid? Since partner will almost certainly bid 2D or 2H, you will only be able to rebid 2S – not a great description of what is, anyway, a meagre hand. Pass describes it much better.

Hand (b) is a lovely opening hand. I would open 1S, but there are those whose Weak Two Openers include 10 and 11pt hands. Here, you can bid 1S, making it harder for your opponents to enter the auction with hearts – if they have them – and you will have no problem with your rebid: a simple 2S. Job done.

The five-card suit is simply not powerful enough to influence you to open on sub-minimum hands, whereas you should certainly be seduced by a half-decent six-card suit. Personally, I recommend that your Weak Two range should be 5–9pts and include really bad 10pt hands. Anything better, like hand (b), needs to be opened with 1S.

So, when you see a six-card suit of even reasonable quality, it is a big asset to your hand or, if it comes to it, as dummy.

Once you start to think about what you are doing, and why, and discard those old fables and tales handed down by dodgy friends and elderly relatives, you will begin to enjoy your bridge so much more. Naturally, pick a group of players who are friendly and interested. If you stop to think and everyone at the table starts yawning and tapping their fingers, you are with the wrong group. I once attended a private class of four very dynamic ladies. While one played the hand, the dummy started doing her online shopping. When it came to analysing the hand at the end, she really didn't know what was more important: her bidding that led to a missed slam or the fact that, this week, bagged carrots were 20p cheaper than loose. It was a long afternoon . . .

When you do play with friends, keep the cards, in duplicate or set-hand style, so that, at the end of the hand, you can take a quick look, review the bidding, the opening lead, the defence and the card play. It needn't be a chore, and it shouldn't be an opportunity for someone to start preaching, but, without doubt, reviewing the hand is incredibly beneficial. Once you can see what you should have done, you'll have a chance on the next hand to do it.

CHAPTER TWO

BIDDING

MY OWN SYSTEM is Acol-based, with a Weak NT and various conventions and gadgets, but each of the following ideas should help you whatever system you play, and whether you are playing socially, at a club, or competitively. As ever, the intention is not to introduce difficult arrangements, but to simplify understandings so that you have more accuracy and cut out the mistakes.

Let's start with some very basic, but absolutely crucial, bridge thinking, included only because, as I travel around bridge clubs, I still see players making life so difficult for themselves.

With a long minor suit, always think about no-trumps

Whenever you hold a long minor suit, a no-trump contact should be in your thoughts, but especially when your partner has opened 1NT; in these examples, partner's 1NT is 12–14pts.

	(a)	(b)	(c)
♠	K9	Q8	10
♥	J106	K5	J93
♦	J95	AQJ974	73
♣	AKJ74	962	AKQJ843

All these hands should, in response to 1NT, bid 3NT immediately. They are all what our American friends might call 'no-brainers'.

The reason is simple: 5C or 5D require eleven tricks; 3NT nine. At Duplicate Pairs, an overtrick in 3NT will outscore 5C or 5D. Even when 3NT might not make, the defence may not find the best defence. If everything goes wrong, you may not make 3NT, but you almost certainly would not have been making 5C or 5D either.

Since you don't want to play with a minor suit as trumps, don't even mention it.

The value of tens – and length – in no-trumps

In no-trump contracts, you want your hands to be heavy in queens, jacks, tens and nines. (In suit contracts, you want aces, kings and singletons.) The reason why you sometimes stop in 1NT and make nine tricks, and, indeed, bid 3NT and go down, is very often that the texture of the hands is unsuitable for a no-trump contract.

Count half a point for each ten you have in your hand when considering playing in a no-trump contract. This is because the 'undergrowth' – as a friend of mine calls it – contributes so much to no-trump contracts, helping to form extra stoppers and create extra tricks.

Also, add one point to your hand for every card you have over four in a long suit, providing it is of decent quality. Generally, if I have, say, a five-card suit including a ten, I just add 1pt for the length and not a half-point for the ten as well.

	(a)		(b)		(c)
♠	J108	♠	AJ3	♠	AJ10
♥	K7	♥	K542	♥	K985
♦	J104	♦	K43	♦	K103
♣	AQ1095	♣	K62	♣	K92

(a) Easily good enough to open 1NT, this hand is worth about 13pts if played in a no-trump contract.

(b) About as nasty a 14pt hand as you could wish for in no-trumps.

(c) Too strong to open 1NT. This hand should be opened with 1H and followed by a rebid of 1NT (or higher if pushed there by partner) showing 15/16pts.

Responding 1NT denies three-card support for partner's major suit

This is such a simple understanding, yet if you can agree this with your partner, it will make your bidding much simpler.

Playing a Weak NT, when you open 1S, you will have a five-card suit about 97 per cent of the time (with two four-card suits including spades, you will always open the lower-ranking one), so supporting with a weak hand and three cards should be standard. However, even in response to a 1H opening, which is more likely to be only a four-card suit, it is still logical and positive when holding a weak hand to support with three cards: you make it harder for your opponents to enter the auction.

If your partner opened 1H, what would you respond?

(a)	(b)
♠ J74	♠ Q97
♥ K72	♥ 542
♦ 84	♦ Q104
♣ K8532	♣ QJ98

(a) Definitely 2H. You have three decent trumps and a doubleton for ruffs.

(b) 1NT. You have three-card heart support but it is your worst suit; your values are all NT orientated (queens, jacks, tens and nines) and your hand is completely balanced.

However, if partner opens 1S, you should respond 2S with both these hands.

So, unless your hand is totally flat and your three-card trump support is lousy, always raise 1H to 2H with a weak hand and, whatever your shape, always raise 1S to 2S with three-card support and a weak hand.

When opener holds a five-card major he knows that, if you respond 1NT, your side won't have an eight-card fit (or if you do have eight hearts between you, your partner's hand is completely flat and won't yield any ruffs). Therefore, partner will have a six-card suit if he rebids his suit after your 1NT response.

Responding at the 2-level

If you play a Strong NT, or a non-Acol-based system, you may have to be strong to change the suit at the 2-level. However, playing a Weak NT system, you are permitted to change the suit at the 2-level with as few as 8pts – high-card points.

The deciding factor as to whether or not to bid at the 2-level should be based less on the length of the suit you are planning to bid and more on whether or not you have tolerance, or some modest support, for the suit your partner initially opened.

Partner opens 1S, and you hold the following hands. What do you respond?

	(a)	(b)	(c)
♠	4	Q8	–
♥	Q7	42	QJ109754
♦	J864	AQ974	Q85
♣	KQ7532	8642	975

(a) 1NT. You hate your partner's spade suit and, despite your six-card club suit, you will get your partner over-excited if you respond 2C.

(b) 2D. This time, you have a doubleton honour in partner's suit so, if he rebids spades, you will not be unhappy. Also, you have a doubleton heart, meaning that if your partner plays in spades, he will have the potential to ruff in your hand with the short trump suit.

(c) 1NT. You want to play with hearts as trumps, but you do not want to get your partner excited. When your partner rebids 2S (as he may well do) you can then bid 3H.

To respond 1NT and then, over opener's rebid, to bid a new suit, shows a very weak hand with a six- or seven-card suit, where you want to play with that suit as trumps. Opener almost always passes.

Shortages are useful in the hand with the shorter trump holding

When you play a hand with a trump suit, you want to make ruffs in the hand which has the shorter trump holding, thus preserving your trump length to draw out your opponents' trumps. You do not want to trump in the hand with the long trumps, since this will just shorten your holding, possibly leading to you being unable to draw the opponents' trumps.

So, when you are supporting your partner, outside shortages are great; when you are the one with the trump length, outside shortages reduce trick loss, but rarely contribute to extra tricks.

Your opponent opens 1H. Would you overcall 2D on this hand?

♠ J42
♥ 7
♦ AQ743
♣ K532

'I had a singleton heart; it makes my hand so much better.' No, regrettably, it doesn't, because trumping hearts in your hand will just shorten your trumps and take you out of control. You have a lousy five-card suit, way weaker than required for an overcall at the 2-level, which should show a hand on which you would have opened the bidding.

That's why a take-out double is such a lovely bid. Opponent opens 1S:

♠ 2

♥ KJ87

♦ AQ72

♣ K532

You double and, whatever your partner responds, you have support and your singleton spade will be in dummy, ready for partner to use for ruffing.

Don't over-value shortages in hands where your trumps will be the long holding.

Your right-hand opponent opens 1H. Do you overcall 1S on these hands?

(a)	(b)
♠ QJ1065	♠ KJ985
♥ 7	♥ 7432
♦ AJ94	♦ A2
♣ 863	♣ 95

Yes, with both, because overcalling 1S always obstructs your opponents, especially if partner can support you.

However, hand (a) is not as suitable as hand (b) because you have a heart shortage and that means that if your opponents lead hearts, as they may well do, you will be trumping in your own hand, shortening your own trumps. In hand (b), if they lead hearts, it will be your partner who is short and you will be able to trump in dummy, creating extra tricks, and ensuring that the hand plays more smoothly. Just bear this in mind the next time you overcall.

Opening the bidding

I know this is almost insultingly basic, but trust me, it really will help you. There are so many lousy guidelines as to when you should open the bidding and no aide-mémoire will ever cater for the myriad exceptions. However, for players of Acol-based Weak NT systems, this one works best:

Open the bidding only with 12 high-card points, unless you have a six-card suit or longer.

This emphasizes the value of a six-card suit, incorporates pre-empts and Weak Twos (if you play them), and stops you from opening on lousy 10 and 11pt hands containing a weedy five-card suit.

And, yes, of course there are exceptions:

(a)

♠ KQJ87

♥ KQ986

♦ 65

♣ 3

Obviously, you can open 1S on this hand – all your points are in your long suits and you have no problem rebidding.

Equally obviously, I hope, you shouldn't open the bidding on this hand:

(b)

♠ 42

♥ K632

♦ Q7432

♣ AQ

If you open 1D on this collection, your partner will respond 1S or 2C and you will be completely stuck. Either you will have to rebid 2D, which is horrible, or you will bid 2H, which is a reverse bid indicating 16pts or more – ludicrous. Just pass and enter the auction later if your opponents locate a fit.

Points

I'll keep it quick.

(a) Points in long suits are worth far more than points in short suits.

(b) Points opposite shortages are wasted.

(c) Points in your partner's suit(s) are much more valuable than points in unbid suits, or your opponents' suit(s).

Take a look at this auction, and these two possible West hands:

(a)	(b)		
West	West	West	East
♠ KQJ4	♠ A742	–	1D
♥ KQJ983	♥ A96432	1H	2C
♦ J3	♦ K3	3H	4C
♣ 3	♣ Q	?	

East is definitely 5-5 in the minor suits, probably 6-5, and holds one heart or none, (East would raise to 4H with a doubleton heart, or even, possibly, with a singleton honour in hearts).

(a) From East's point of view, if playing the contract, the only card with any value in West's hand is J♦. If East has a singleton heart and a singleton spade, none of West's other values are of any use to East whatsoever. West should probably bid 4H now, and try to play the hand.

(b) All West's points are working. His two major suit aces will cover any losers in those suits and he has both K♦ and Q♣, both of which

25

will bring a big smile to East's face. Bidding 5 (as a cue-bid), 6D, or even 4NT all seem reasonable now, depending upon your style.

The value of your hand changes throughout the auction and you must be alert to this in order to assess the best contract. Responding to pre-empts and big two-suited hands (as above) only aces in the outside suits are likely to be valuable. Any points in partner's long suit(s) will be very valuable.

Opposite a Weak 3 opener, only aces and connected kings will be useful to partner, apart from points you may hold in his suit.

Opening 1NT with a five-card major suit

I am asked about this often because a few eminent – one might almost say pre-eminent – teachers recommend this to their students.

If your aim is to be a relaxed, fun, social bridge player, then opening 1NT with a five-card major suit is just fine. Read no more of this killjoy little section.

However, if you have ambitions to be better, I strongly suggest that you never open 1NT with a five-card major suit. If your suit is strong, it will play just as well in no-trumps as in the major and, if your suit quality is bad, then you definitely want it as a trump suit since to establish it in no-trumps may take some doing.

If you want convincing that opening 1H or 1S with a five-card major suit is the right action, ask yourself why you would always make a weak take-out (or Transfer) after your partner's 1NT opening if you held a five-card suit? It's because five-card major suits play better as trumps.

And, yes, you will end up playing in 5-1 and 5-2 fits and they won't all be pleasant. But bridge isn't a pleasant game: most of the time, it's hell (but we like it).

Shape showing

The essence of good bidding is to describe your shape and point count. Balanced hands are easily represented by no-trump opening bids and rebids, but two-suited hands sometimes cause problems:

1H	1S
2C	

In modern Acol-style bidding, the above shows at least five hearts and four clubs.

1H	1S
2C	2NT
3C	

The rebid of the second suit confirms five of them, so this shows five hearts and five clubs.

1H	1S
2C	2NT
4C	

This shows six hearts and five clubs. To bypass 3NT should always suggest at least 6-5 in your two suits (see page 33).

Where a 'reverse' sequence occurs, the bigger two-suited hands can be shown even more easily:

1H	2C
2S	2NT
3S	

Since the opener has bid spades twice, he must have five of them. As, with 5-5 in spades and hearts, one would open 1S first, the opener must be showing six hearts and five spades.

Notice that in all these examples, to show a two-suited hand of 5-5 or longer, you open the appropriate suit and never bid it again. By bidding your second suit repeatedly, your second suit gets longer and then, automatically, you must be showing extra length in your first suit, since you chose to open it first.

With two five-card suits, open the higher-ranking, except if you have spades and clubs, when opening 1C will prove more economical. Some players opt to open 1S with 5-5 in clubs and spades but I remain mystified as to why – in the long run – this will work better. In my experience, opening 1C on 5-5 hands with spades and clubs works beautifully, as does opening 1C on 6-6 hands.

Fourth Suit Forcing

In an uncontested auction, there is no better way to encourage your partner to show his or her shape than by using Fourth Suit Forcing (4SF).

When you and your partner have bid three suits, if you have good cards in the unbid suit, with sufficient points to bid game, then you should bid 3NT. However, when you do not hold two stoppers in the fourth suit, or you think you may be too strong to bid 3NT, you can employ 4SF.

West		West	East
♠ AJ864		–	1H
♥ Q4		1S	2C
♦ Q52		**2D**	
♣ AJ7			

Your bid of the fourth suit shows an opening hand or better (unless your partner has guaranteed extra points by, for example, a reverse sequence), and you are suggesting that you have half a stopper or one stopper in the fourth suit. Now, you demand that your partner describes his hand further:

With a stopper in the fourth suit, he rebids no-trumps (2NT with 12/13pts, 3NT with 14pts or more).

This is the most common use for 4SF – to find help in the fourth suit and then play in a no-trump contract. However, if partner does not have a stopper in the fourth suit, he has a variety of other shape-showing bids to make:

With 5-5 in his two suits, he bids his second suit again.

With 6-5 in his two suits, he jump-bids his second suit (probably bypassing 3NT – see below).

With 6-4 in his two suits, unless he is a minimum opener, he jump-bids his first suit.

With three-card support for your suit, here spades, he jumps to 3S. This shows: five hearts, four clubs, three spades and therefore, only one diamond. It is my favourite 4SF rebid since 5-4-3-1 is the ideal shape to have in dummy.

West		East
♠ Q82		♠ AKJ54
♥ 6	N	♥ J103
	W E	
♦ AQ832	S	♦ K74
♣ AK92		♣ J7

West	East
1D	1S
2C	2H*
3S	4NT
5S	**6S**

* 4SF

West describes his hand correctly and an excellent slam contract is reached, impossible without East knowing that West holds a singleton heart. West's 5S response to 4NT is Roman Key-Card Blackwood, showing two key-cards and the trump queen, definitely an improvement on traditional Blackwood.

Notice that to show three-card spade support, West must jump to 3S. The reason for this is that to bid 2S would show something different.

With two-card support for your major suit, here spades, including an honour card, partner rebids 2S. This shows 5-4-2-2, without a stopper in the fourth suit.

This last description is usually not known or remembered by players, but can prove very useful, as in the hand below:

West		East
♠ Q8		♠ KJ1094
♥ 62	N	♥ K53
♦ KQ832	W E	♦ A4
♣ AK92	S	♣ J75

West	East
1D	1S
2C	2H*
2S	**4S**

* 4SF

Following the 4SF bid, West's bid of 2S indicates a doubleton honour in spades and, here, allows East to bid 4S, knowing that West holds ♠Ax or ♠Qx (x = 9, or lower), staying out of the inferior 3NT contract.

West		East
♠ Q8		♠ A7432
♥ 62	N	♥ K103
♦ KQ832	W E	♦ A4
♣ AK92	S	♣ Q75

West	East
1D	1S
2C	2H*
2S	**3NT**

* 4SF

Now, when East holds spades which are unlikely to play well opposite a doubleton honour, he can opt for 3NT, which offers myriad possibilities to make.

Talk to your partner about Fourth Suit Forcing to ensure that you both have the same agreements. Bridge is a tough enough game without succumbing to conventional misunderstandings.

Unilateral bypass of 3NT

This sounds complex but is really very simple and totally logical. If you and your partner(s) have the same understanding, it will make your lives much easier.

If one member of your side unilaterally jumps past 3NT this signifies at least 6-5 in his two suits. You will never bypass 3NT if you are merely 5-5, since this distribution may still work well for a no-trump contract. This ensures that a deal such as this is easily bid:

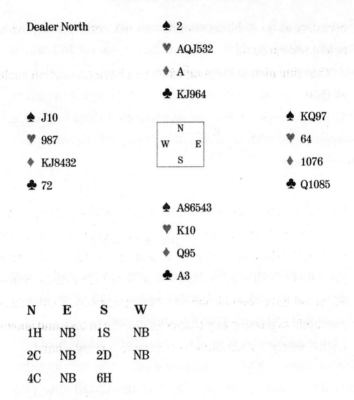

Dealer North

North			
♠ 2			
♥ AQJ532			
♦ A			
♣ KJ964			

West		East
♠ J10		♠ KQ97
♥ 987		♥ 64
♦ KJ8432		♦ 1076
♣ 72		♣ Q1085

South			
♠ A86543			
♥ K10			
♦ Q95			
♣ A3			

N	E	S	W
1H	NB	1S	NB
2C	NB	2D	NB
4C	NB	6H	

South's 2D bid is Fourth Suit Forcing, asking for further hand description from North. When North jumps to 4C, by-passing 3NT, this should show not simply a strong 5-5 hand, but instead the more distributional 6-5 shape. Now, South can value up his good holdings in both North's suits and, although approaching the slam scientifically is now quite difficult, if all else fails, South can certainly punt it – which is what happened at the table. Very few pairs reached 6H because, at most tables, South was not certain that North held a six-card suit.

This rule also holds good when you have an auction such as this:

N	E	S	W
–	–	1H	1S
2D	NB	4C	

Unless 4C is a Splinter bid agreeing diamonds (many people only play Splinters in response to a major suit bid – and, after intervention, only in the opponents' bid suit) then South's jump to 4C is showing a 6-5 hand in hearts and clubs. Since 3C would have been strong and forcing anyway, South is deliberately bypassing any chance of playing in 3NT and showing his wildly distributional – and game-forcing – hand.

Bid your weaker minor suit on the way to 3NT

When opening a balanced hand with two four-card suits, I generally play that it is right to open 1H if you have hearts and, without a heart suit, whatever you like as long as it isn't spades. But, with what would you open the bidding with this hand?

♠ QJ4
♥ A2
♦ AKQ2
♣ 6532

Playing a Strong NT, I guess you open 1NT but, playing a Weak NT, your plan is to bid a four-card suit and then rebid no-trumps at the lowest available level. For this reason, I would open 1C on this hand . . . and 1D on the hand below:

♠ A3
♥ AQ3
♦ 7532
♣ AQ107

When you are planning on playing in no-trumps, opening a weak suit to dissuade your opponents from leading it can prove a very profitable exercise. If your partner supports you, you can pass with 15/16pts and rebid no-trumps with 17–20pts; if he insists on playing with your minor as trumps, then presumably he has shape and the contract will play just fine, and if you end up in no-trumps and gain the tempo because your opponents didn't lead your minor, then you will make contracts that would normally have failed.

Further, just because your opponents know that you open your weaker four-card minor suit doesn't mean they will know when you are doing it. Any auction when you open a minor and then rebid no-trumps could feature a five- or six-card minor suit.

Finally, if you are heading towards a slam, I recommend bidding your strongest suits at all times. At the 5-level and above, it is far more useful to know where your partner's values lie than to try to put your opponent off the best lead (although there are some experts who specialize in that sort of thing).

Next up, a small, but vital, partnership understanding which should be part of everyone's repertoire:

Hand descriptions showing three-card support for partner's major suit

One of the most challenging situations for a responder to an opening bid is whether to emphasize their five-card major suit, whether to show preference or to move towards 3NT, perhaps losing the eight-card fit. One agreement which simplifies this problem is as follows:

Never open a minor suit and make a minimum rebid of that minor if you have three-card support for your partner's major suit.

Hence,

1C	1S
2C	

denies three-card spade support, and now responder can move forward knowing that a 5-3 fit is not available in spades.

1C	1S
2S	

only promises three-card spade support, a minimum hand, and does not deny a six-card club suit.

1C	1S
3C	

does not deny three-card spade support; you are likely to be able to show this feature later.

This leads to this situation:

(a)	**(b)**
♠ Q65	♠ QJ8
♥ 7	♥ 6
♦ AJ943	♦ KQ832
♣ KQ86	♣ AK92

(a) You open 1D and your partner responds 1S. You have a minimum opening hand, and it is right to support your partner immediately. This will ensure that you play in 2S when your partner holds a weak hand with a five-card suit, and will also guide you towards the most likely game contract.

(b) You open 1D and your partner responds 1S. Here, your hand is stronger and game may be available even opposite a weak hand containing five spades. So, it is better to rebid 2C and, whatever partner bids next, jump to 3S subsequently. This shows a strong 5-4-3-1 shape and will allow partner to judge the final contract effectively.

Simply, if you are weak, support partner's major suit immediately. With stronger hands, you can develop the auction and show the three-card spade (or heart) support subsequently.

The top priority for responder

The responder to an opening bid of 1-of-a-suit has a solemn duty to perform: he must show any four-card major suit at the 1-level if he can. This is because a 4-4 fit in a major suit is usually the best contract to find, and because the opener cannot always show four-card major suits, since he must show his overall shape and point-count.

When the responder has a strong hand, say a good 11pts or more, he can bid out his hand in the normal way, showing his longer suit first, and then his shorter suit. However, when the responder holds 6–10pts, he may have to show a four-card major suit ahead of a longer minor suit.

If your partner opens 1D, what should you respond on these hands?

(a)	**(b)**
♠ AQ65	♠ KJ74
♥ A7	♥ 96
♦ 43	♦ 32
♣ KJ984	♣ AJ972

(a) With this hand, you can respond 2C and, later, show your four-card spade suit.

(b) With this weaker hand, your responsibility as the responder is to ensure that you bid your four-card major suit, so, despite having longer clubs, you should respond 1S initially.

The way to think about this situation is to imagine that your partner will rebid his original suit, showing a minimum opening hand. Opposite this rebid, you are only strong enough to show a second suit when you hold at least 11pts. So, when you hold less than 11pts, you must show your major suit ahead of a longer minor suit as you are not strong enough to bid a second suit if your partner rebids his original suit.

If your partner rebids a new second suit, you can then bid no-trumps to indicate that you hold good cards in the unbid suit. If you happen to have five of them – as you do in hand (b), then that will be an asset to you playing in a no-trump contract.

5-4-3-1: the ideal shape for dummy

There is really nothing nicer than to see this shape of hand as dummy – providing, of course, that the singleton isn't the trump suit.

I say there is nothing nicer, but a 6-4-2-1, or 7-4-2-0 shape is likely to be even better – if a great deal rarer.

If we look specifically at the 5-4-3-1 shape, providing that the three- or four-card holding is trumps, you now have a singleton with which to make ruffs and a five-card suit which may be establishable. These two elements represent the two features with which you make extra tricks, and this shape provides both opportunities.

I cannot stress enough how much more useful shortages are when they are contained in the hand with the shorter, or weaker, trump holding. Shortages in the hand in which the long trumps are located are never as useful, restricting losers as opposed to generating extra tricks.

To illustrate this, take a standard situation such as the following. Your right-hand opponent opens the bidding with 1S. Would you prefer to hold hand (a) or hand (b)?

	(a)		**(b)**
♠	5	♠	J842
♥	KJ7	♥	6
♦	AQJ86	♦	AQJ86
♣	Q862	♣	AJ2

Hand (a) presents some problems. You are just about good enough to make an overcall of 2D, but you do not really want to play there since the opposition will start off with spades and immediately force you to ruff in your own hand. To make a take-out double may be better, but you only have three hearts, which may disappoint your partner. At least if you do double, your hand is likely to be dummy should your side get to play the contract – and that will work better.

Hand (b) is also a slim hand on which to overcall 2D but at least this time if you do play in diamonds and your opponents lead spades, partner is likely to be short and so you can ruff in dummy.

This is assuming that there is some kind of fit on this hand. Unfortunately, it may be a misfit hand. I think if I were vulnerable, I would be happy to pass on this collection and see what happens next.

The best way of locating a 5-4-3-1 hand is via Fourth Suit Forcing and it involves one of my favourite sequences in the whole game:

West		East
♠ AK965		♠ 43
♥ A952	N	♥ K6
♦ Q97	W E	♦ AK8643
♣ 8	S	♣ A53

This hand came up in random play just this morning and shows how perfectly the two hands fit together.

West	East
1S	2D
2H	3C*
3D	

*4SF

West's first three bids are wonderfully descriptive of his hand. The auction can then continue:

	4NT
5S	5NT
6S	**7D**

When East uses Fourth Suit Forcing, he is still uncertain as to what the final contract might be. If West rebids 3NT, indicating a stopper in clubs, that may end the auction. As it is, when West rebids 3D, he indicates five spades, four hearts, three diamonds and, at most, a singleton club. This shape is ideal for East and, holding predominantly suit-orientated values – aces and kings – he can be optimistic about slam potential. His knowledge that West holds a singleton club means that missing K♣, Q♣ and J♣ is no loss, as he can ruff two clubs in the West hand if required.

It would be nice to check that West held a top card in spades, but launching into Blackwood, or here, Roman Key-Card Blackwood, is quite reasonable since West's values are almost certainly in hearts and spades.

West's 5S response shows two key-cards, plus the trump queen. East can see a loser in spades, none in hearts or diamonds, and two losers in clubs which can be ruffed. Therefore, if West holds K♠ also, the grand slam may be available. 5NT asks West to name the suit in which he holds a king (other than the trump king, which was already included in the initial RKCB response). When West bids 6S, East bids 7D with confidence and the excellent grand slam is massively odds-on to succeed.

Fit jumps

Mainly used in competitive auctions (although there is one non-competitive time when it is very useful too, at which we will look in a moment), this is a fabulous shape-showing tool, very helpful in deciding how high to compete, whether to make sacrifices and whether or not your opponents are likely to make what they have just bid.

These bids are also excellent to learn as they reinforce the idea that when you have a fit with your partner you can bid up, and when you don't, you should stay out of the action: such a simple principle, which everyone probably thinks that they know, but one which I see broken time and time again, day after day . . .

The principle is this: if, in a competitive auction (or the one exception below) you jump in a new suit opposite your partner's opening bid or overcall, you are showing a fit with his suit and a good-quality five- or six-card suit of your own. The bid is usually played as non-forcing and relatively weak in strength.

Here's that exception:

West	East
NB	1D
2H	

Having passed, if you jump in a new suit, most good players these days assume that this is a Fit jump. The standard understanding of Fit jumps is that they are relatively weak, showing support for partner's suit and a decent-quality five-card suit (or longer) of your own. Often, the support for partner is poor quality and, if partner finds himself on lead, he should opt for your suit, rather than under-leading honours in his own suit.

West might have a hand such as these:

(a)	(b)
♠ 65	♠ 2
♥ AKJ97	♥ KQJ984
♦ Q1054	♦ 1083
♣ 86	♣ K92

If you play Weak Two openers in the major suits, partner will not hold hand (b), since he would have opened 2H initially. However, if you do not play Weak Two opening bids, then a Fit jump does show either a five- or six-card suit.

However, he may hold hand (a). The advantage of making the Fit jump here is that it may dissuade opponents from entering the auction and, if they do, partner can judge whether to bid on or defend. In simple terms, if you have high cards in your partner's suit, these are valuable; if you hold high cards in the unbid suits, they are less valuable.

As always, length in partner's suit – here, a fit in two suits – is likely to yield extra tricks and provides a very good reason to bid on.

In competitive auctions, Fit jumps will provide crucial distributional information to help partner to judge what action to take at high levels. The principle is that you will not necessarily jump merely one level, but to as high a level as you believe it is sensible for your side to be. You should not jump to game in a new suit, however, as this would be a natural bid where you intend to play in the game contract.

FIT JUMPS AFTER A TAKE-OUT DOUBLE

If you have a fit with your partner and there is an intervening take-out double, you know that your opponents are on the way to finding their own fit. For this reason, when you are weak with four-card support for partner's suit, you jump to attempt to pre-empt your opponents out of the auction.

The use of a Fit jump in this situation can be used to establish whether your side holds a double fit, how high to compete or when to double. Let's take a look at a deal where the Fit jump proved particularly useful.

Dealer South	♠ 4	
E/W Game	♥ J865	
	♦ AJ9743	
	♣ 106	

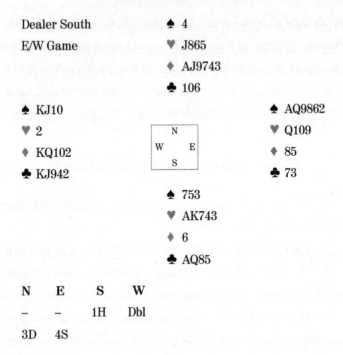

	♠ KJ10				♠ AQ9862
	♥ 2		N		♥ Q109
	♦ KQ102	W		E	♦ 85
	♣ KJ942		S		♣ 73

	♠ 753
	♥ AK743
	♦ 6
	♣ AQ85

N	E	S	W
–	–	1H	Dbl
3D	4S		

North's jump to 3D indicated a weak hand with a raise to 3H, including a five- or six-card diamond suit of decent quality. East overdid his jump to 4S – his ♥Q109 are likely to be completely wasted. Holding a singleton diamond, South knew that the hands were not fitting that well and he found it easy to pass. North, having described his hand beautifully the first time, could also pass.

On the lead of 6♦, South made a diamond ruff and two aces to defeat 4S when 4H was almost always not making and 5H was certainly failing.

This was a real deal in which several South players ended up in 5H, scoring badly. But, if we change the hand a little, we can see when it would have been right to bid on.

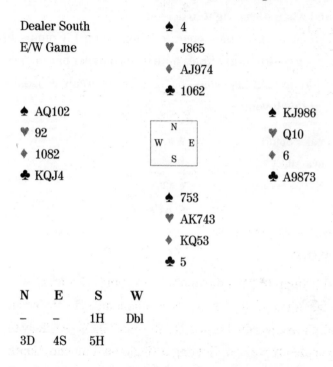

Dealer South
E/W Game

```
              ♠ 4
              ♥ J865
              ♦ AJ974
              ♣ 1062
♠ AQ102                      ♠ KJ986
♥ 92            N            ♥ Q10
♦ 1082      W       E        ♦ 6
♣ KQJ4          S            ♣ A9873
              ♠ 753
              ♥ AK743
              ♦ KQ53
              ♣ 5
```

N	E	S	W
–	–	1H	Dbl
3D	4S	5H	

Now, South has a fit with partner's diamonds and when East bids 4S this time, it should be reasonably easy for South to bid 5H. He probably does not expect to make it, but holding a double fit often produces extra tricks and so it is here: 5H makes and so, incidentally, does 4S, mainly because both sides have a double fit.

Compare the two South hands and see how, without the Fit jump from North, South could never differentiate between the two hands and judge when it was correct to bid on and when it was right to defend.

The same principles operate when using Fit jumps in other competitive situations, both when partner has opened the bidding, and also when partner has overcalled. Take a look at this layout:

Dealer South	♠ 4	
Love All	♥ K865	
	♦ 43	
	♣ K106532	

♠ AK1086		♠ QJ92
♥ Q10	N	♥ 92
♦ J102	W E	♦ AQ987
♣ Q87	S	♣ 94

	♠ 753
	♥ AJ743
	♦ K65
	♣ AJ

N	E	S	W
–	–	1H	1S
4C	4S	?	

North's jump to 4C indicated a weak hand which North felt was worth a raise to 4H, including a decent-quality five- or six-card club suit. With one less club and one more spade, for example, he could have jumped to 3C.

The Fit jump should always promise four-card support opposite an opening bid (unless your opener guarantees a five-card suit), and the suit in which the jump is made should promise one of the two top honours.

When East bids 4S, South is faced with a typical high-level decision. Here, he can reason that North is likely to hold a singleton spade and that, if he also holds five or six clubs headed by K♣, there is a good chance of establishing the long suit and pitching diamond losers. 5H therefore looks make-able and South duly bids it. East-West should take A♠ and A♦ but, with the trumps dividing 2-2, South can set up dummy's clubs on which to discard his other diamond losers.

This is a good result for North-South since, if they had doubled East's 4S, West would come to eight tricks, losing only 300pts, instead of 450pts.

Could this 4C bid be confused with a Splinter?

The answer should be no because, once your opponents have started bidding, you should limit Splinter bids to be used only in your opponents' suit and not in a new suit. Here, South did not really need North to tell him that he had a singleton spade because the auction strongly suggests this anyway. What is useful is knowing that North holds a decent-quality five- or six-card club suit headed by one of the top two honours which South can work out can be established.

In competitive auctions, only Splinter in your opponents' suit; a jump in a new suit will be a Fit jump.

Fit jumps can also be used when your partner has overcalled.

Dealer East	♠ J4	
E/W Game	♥ 7653	
	♦ AJ10643	
	♣ 6	

♠ 10982		♠ AKQ53
♥ 942		♥ 8
♦ K7		♦ 85
♣ Q954		♣ AK1073

	♠ 76	
	♥ AKQJ10	
	♦ Q92	
	♣ J82	

N	E	S	W
–	1S*	2H	2S
4D	4S	?	

* Many, including me, would open 1C.

North's Fit jump to 4D is certainly aggressive but, being so weak, he expects East to bid 4S and, at this vulnerability, he wants South to be able to make an informed decision about the sacrifice. South, holding three cards in diamonds, is now happy to take the risk of bidding at the 5-level. 5H doubled is only one down, whereas 4S is making and 5S is down if South leads a top heart followed by a diamond switch, preferably, Q♦.

You may ask how it is possible that both sides can make ten tricks on the same hand. The answer lies in the double fit which is held by both sides: what is generally called a 'double, double fit'. Both sides have two nine-card suits and that strongly suggests that twenty tricks are likely to be made between the two partnerships. For devotees of the Law of Total Tricks, you are adding one extra trump onto both sides' longest suits because of the double fit and this makes the total of likely tricks equal twenty.

Incidentally, I have a simple rule to judge whether or not to bid at the 5-level in these situations:

Never bid at the 5-level in a competitive auction without at least ten trumps between you and your partner, unless you hold a fit in two suits (a double fit).

So, to conclude:

A Fit jump is a weak style of bid, generally 4–10pts,

designed to assist partner in judging competitive levels. It will improve accuracy enormously and cut down on high-level guessing.

A Fit jump guarantees that your side holds at least an eight-card fit in the first suit bid. The Fit-jumper will generally hold four-card support for opener's bid. In response to an overcall, a Fit jump at the 2- or 3-level promises at least three-card support; at the 4-level, it will promise at least four-card support.

The suit in which you make the jump will be of decent quality and contain at least five cards, headed by one of the top two honours.

Since you should agree with your partner that you will only make Splinter bids in a competitive auction in your opponents' suit, there should be no confusion about which bid is which.

In competition, any jump to game in a new suit is to play, and it will not be a Fit Jump.

Fit non-jumps

Really?

Yes. Although you actually have no need ever to call these bids by their proper name, you and your partner should have an agreement as to what these sequences imply.

	(a)		
N	E	S	W
1H	1S	2C	**2D**

	(b)		
N	E	S	W
1H	2C	NB	**2S**

In sequence (a), East overcalls 1S and, when South responds 2C, West freely enters the auction and changes the suit. The fact that there is no need whatsoever for West to bid here suggests that the hand is fitting. West is promising some support for partner's spades and also a five-card diamond suit of decent quality. I would expect the West hand to look something like this:

West

♠ J43

♥ 32

♦ AQJ64

♣ 654

There is no need for West to raise spades with three such poor cards, but he can show limited support for spades, plus decent diamonds by making a Fit non-jump. If West held no support for spades, he should stay out of the auction.

The advantage of bidding 2D here is that partner can now compete further with six spades, support for diamonds, or five spades and three-card diamond support. On top of this, if East is on lead – and if North-South play in hearts, he will be – he can now lead a diamond safely rather than speculating on a spade lead.

In auction (b), West faces a different situation. South has passed and, if he passes also, the auction may end. He is changing from a minor suit to a major suit opposite a 2-level overcall. Here, the bid is more forced and, as a result, this bid does not promise any support for partner's minor suit. West may have:

West

♠ AQJ97

♥ A32

♦ 964

♣ 65

To pass when partner might hold 14pts would be to risk missing a game contract. Without support for partner's suit, changing suit at the 2-level, without jumping, is ample, and partner should consider such action constructive, raising you with three-card support.

If your partner overcalls, the basic rule is 'support or shut up'.

If you change suit after an opponent has bid between your partner's overcall and your response, you are suggesting moderate support for partner, with a high-quality five- or six-card suit of your own. Without support for partner's suit, simply pass.

This advice may be simple, but it works remarkably well in the vast majority of situations.

Defending Weak Twos

So many people play Weak Two openers now, yet, in my experience, many play them without knowing them fluently. This leads to partnership errors and affects your confidence in your partner. Check that your partnership knows the meaning of all the possible responses to a Weak Two opener.

More importantly, partnerships do not seem to know the best ways to defend against Weak Two openers when they are used by their opponents. So, in this section, I want to establish some key factors so that you can tackle your aggressive opponents effectively and with a minimum of complex understandings. The principles here will also apply when you come to other competitive situations which involve conventional bids from your opponents.

I teach my students to play Weak Two openers just in the major suits, but many people now play Weak Twos in three and even all four suits. Their big advantage is that they use up an enormous amount of bidding space with relatively little risk. In order to give yourself a chance against them you and your partner must understand some key principles.

MAKE A STRONG BID OVER A WEAK BID;
MAKE A WEAK BID OVER A STRONG BID

This is a key principle in competitive bidding. Over your opponents' strong bids, your aim should be to obstruct their auction; therefore, calling on weak, distributional hands is desirable. With a decent hand yourself, sitting over a strong bid by an opponent, be cautious: your partner may have nothing; your limit is likely to be no more than a part-score, so risk should be avoided.

Over a weak bid, all your bids should be strong, whatever your standard system. In these situations, your side hopes to buy the contract. To do this, you must provide an accurate idea of your hand to your partner, describe distribution well, and remain aware that a pre-empt from an opponent usually heralds poor distribution. These are all reasons why you should resist overcalling on marginal hands.

AN OVERCALL AFTER A WEAK TWO IS STRONG

The key to successful overcalling after a Weak Two is to ensure that you have a robust opening hand with a five- or six-card suit of good quality. Don't be tempted to bid light just because you don't want your opponents to get away with their pre-empt. Occasionally, their strategy will work and you will miss part-scores you might have made but, usually, some care ensures fewer disastrous – and often doubled – over-bid contracts.

A JUMP-OVERCALL AFTER A WEAK TWO IS STRONG

Whatever style you normally play for your jump-overcalls, over a Weak Two you should play them as strong, based on the principle of not making a weak bid over a weak bid. Some people play jump-overcalls in this situation as showing two-suited hands – and this can prove a useful approach – but, whatever you and your partner do, ensure that you both know your system. If in doubt, keep it simple, and play jump-overcalls over a Weak Two opener as strong. A good guide would be to say they should show about 15–18pts with a high-quality six-card suit.

OVER A PRE-EMPT, A TAKE-OUT DOUBLE SHOWS A GOOD OPENING HAND, WITH ALL THREE UNBID SUITS, OR A TWO-SUITED HAND, IDEALLY 5-5 OR LONGER

Unlike over a 1-level opening bid, when a take-out double should show the three remaining suits or, rarely, a very strong single-suited hand, over a pre-empt you would overcall or jump-overcall with a strong single-suited hand. This leaves a take-out double here to show a two- or three-suited hand.

With a three-suited hand, you will be likely to pass whichever suit your partner names, unless you are considerably stronger than your partner might expect. With a two-suited hand, if partner bids the suit you do not hold, you must then rebid your lower-ranking suit (even if it is shorter in length than the higher-ranking suit), so that partner realizes you have two suits and can pass or adjust to the other suit at the lowest available level.

Dealer East   ♠ A4

N/S Game   ♥ 765

                     ♦ K43

                     ♣ KJ843

	♠ 982			♠ KQJ1053
	♥ Q942	N		♥ 8
	♦ 106	W E		♦ 875
	♣ AQ109	S		♣ 765

                  ♠ 76

                  ♥ AKJ103

                  ♦ AQJ92

                  ♣ 2

N	E	S	W
–	2S	Dbl	NB
4C	NB	4D	NB
4H			

When North responds 4C (he must jump to show a near-opening hand) and South bids a new suit, 4D, North knows that South must have a two-suited hand with diamonds and hearts. Since ten tricks in diamonds does not make game, he opts to convert to 4H.

Note how important is South's 10♥. Despite the likely (after the pre-empt) bad break in trumps, North is still in control, having good-quality trumps. This is why bids over pre-empts should be kept up to good strength.

A BID OF THE WEAK 2 OPENER'S SUIT
SEEKS NO-TRUMPS

Since a Weak Two opener shows a weak hand with a six-card suit, it is quite likely that another player at the table holds a strong hand with a long suit. If that hand belongs to an opponent and his long suit is a minor, he should be seeking a 3NT contract but, with most of his bidding space used up, how can he do this?

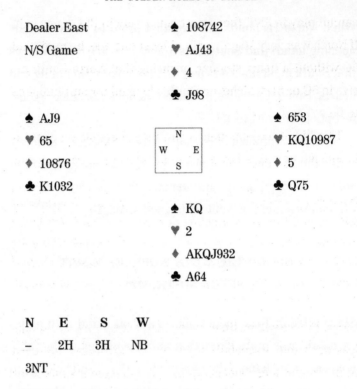

Dealer East
N/S Game

♠ 108742
♥ AJ43
♦ 4
♣ J98

♠ AJ9
♥ 65
♦ 10876
♣ K1032

♠ 653
♥ KQ10987
♦ 5
♣ Q75

♠ KQ
♥ 2
♦ AKQJ932
♣ A64

N	E	S	W
–	2H	3H	NB
3NT			

An immediate cue-bid of a Weak Two opener says: I think I can make 3NT, but I have no stopper in the opponent's suit. If you have one, bid 3NT, partner; if you do not, bid 4C.

It does not matter whether the rest of North's hand is balanced, only that he has a stopper in the opponent's suit. South should have at least eight tricks on his own.

The reason why partner bids 4C without a stopper is, since South's cue-bid is based on a long minor suit, if North cannot play in 3NT, then South must play in the minor suit. If North was very strong, with at least one ace, he might bid 5C without a heart stopper, ensuring that North-South arrive in 5C or 5D whichever South's long minor suit happens to be.

This bid of the opponent's suit may seem strange, but it is consistent with a key principle which has myriad facets:

If you bid your opponents' suit after your partner has already bid – at any time in the auction – at the two or three-level, you are expressing an interest in a game contract and asking for further description from partner: first and foremost, if partner holds a stopper in the opponent's suit, he must rebid no-trumps.

Clearly, there will be times when a no-trump contract seems less desirable, especially if you have shown an eight-card fit in a major suit, but the bid of the opponent's suit serves to force the auction to game.

If you bid your opponents' suit at the four-level or above, you are saying that you love your partner's suit (or the suit you have agreed), you are too good to bid game and wish to investigate for a slam. You are showing the ace or a singleton in the opponents' suit.

For example, you might have an auction such as this one:

N	E	S	W
–	–	1S	2C
3S*	NB	4C	

* 10–12pts

South

♠ AQ7432

♥ AKJ

♦ 93

♣ A6

South's bid of 4C shows a hand too strong to bid 4S, indicating a singleton, void or ace in clubs and asking partner to cue-bid an ace at the 4-level. If East can cue-bid 4D to show A♦, then West has controls in every suit and can proceed towards a slam, perhaps by bidding 4NT (ideally, Roman Key-Card Blackwood) next. If East returns to 4S, West may subside and settle for game.

The law of total tricks

This is a complex principle concerning competitive bidding and the likely number of tricks available to both sides. I have written about the most useful applications of this

'Law' many times and at different standards. Here, I would like to radically précis the complexity to form a simple set of principles about which to think when competing.

When involved in a competitive auction:

- your distribution becomes much more important than your points;
- the number of cards you and your partner have in your best suit is vital;
- the quality of your chosen trump suit is very important.

This is because, in a competitive auction, your aim is to secure a making contract for your side if you can but, at least, to steal a contract cheaply from your opponents and lose fewer points going down than you would have done had they made their contract, or to push them to too high a contract.

The so-called 'Law' of Total Tricks suggests that the number of tricks available for both sides will be, allowing for adjustments and alterations, equal to the cards in the longest suit each side holds added together. In simple terms, if one side has an eight-card fit in hearts, and the other side has an eight-card fit in spades, sixteen tricks can be made if one side plays with their suit as trumps and the other side plays with their suit as trumps. Obviously, both sides can't play with their suit as trumps, but both sides have the potential to do so.

This leads us to the following key principle:

In a competitive auction, assuming decent suit quality, you are safe to bid the same number of tricks as you have trumps and, taking into account vulnerability, up to one trick more than you have cards in your long suit – but no higher.

There is an exception to this rule, which I shall mention in a moment, but this is a really good guide when wondering whether or not to bid on.

In competitive auctions (unless one of you feels that you know there might be a game contract available since you have the clear majority of the points), generally:

- With an eight-card fit with partner, bid to the 3-level and no higher.
- With a nine-card fit, bid to the 4-level and no higher.
- Bid at the 5-level only with at least ten cards between you in your longest suit.

The exception to this rule is when you and your partner hold an eight-card fit or longer in two suits, a so-called 'double fit'. When this occurs, judging the likely number of tricks you will make can be very tough but, generally, you will make one more trick than you might normally expect.

Let's look at the following problems and, using just basic

knowledge of the Law of Total Tricks, see if solutions can
be found:

South

♠ KQ954

♥ A42

♦ 98

♣ A73

N	E	S	W
–	–	1S	2H
2S	3H	?	

You have a minimum hand, but you should never pass. You
and your partner hold an eight- or nine-card fit in spades,
and East-West hold nine hearts. Since you are safe to bid
up to the same level as you have cards in your longest suit,
plus one more, you are safe to compete with 3S.

If you are not making 3S, your opponents may well be
making 3H. If you can make 3S, hooray. Either way, it will
almost always be right to bid 3S.

South

♠ 954

♥ AJ42

♦ KJ8

♣ Q103

N	E	S	W
–	–	–	3S
Dbl	NB	?	

This is typical of the type of problem one often faces. Your partner has shown an opening hand with a shortage in spades: should you bid 4H, or something else?

There is no perfect answer here: your partner might have five bad hearts or four very good ones, the trumps may split nicely and 4H will make. But, usually, it will be better here to pass.

Partner may hold only three hearts but, assuming he has four, you still only have eight cards in your suit, so you should not bid higher than the 3-level. Also, if your partner has 14pts and the trumps break 4-1 which, after a pre-empt, they may well do, you may have no play for the contract whatsoever.

By passing, you are likely to defeat 3S on sheer weight of points, and the stronger your partner is, the more you will receive in penalties.

Of course, the decision will depend somewhat on whether you are playing Duplicate Pairs, Teams-of-Four, or Rubber Bridge, and on the relative vulnerabilities. If you are playing Teams-of-Four or Rubber Bridge, and your side is vulnerable and your opponents are not, you will be more inclined to punt 4H. However, in the long run, pass will prove your best action – and you can be guided by your knowledge of just how important trump length is during competitive auctions.

At low levels, you can distil the understanding to these thoughts:

- If you and your opponents both have an eight-card fit, **one** side should bid at the 3-level.
- If one side holds an eight-card fit and the other a nine-card fit, **both** sides should be prepared to compete at the 3-level.

Often you cannot be certain of your trump length or that of your opponents, but sometimes you can – that is the time to use this understanding to aid your judgement.

If your opponents have an eight-card fit, NEVER (almost never) let them play at the 2-level

I am gobsmacked by how often players who understand this principle still let their opponents have an easy time.

If your opponents have an eight-card fit then your side will almost always have an eight-card fit also. If you both have an eight-card fit, one of you should bid at the 3-level. If you fail by one trick, that will be better than letting your opponents make their contract. And, of course, you could persuade your opponents to bid on to the 3-level themselves. If they do that and make it, they were too strong for you; if they fail, you have foiled them in their attempt to make a quiet part-score.

South

♠ 954

♥ AJ4

♦ 86

♣ QJ1032

N	E	S	W
–	1S	NB	2S
NB	NB	?	

Your opponents have eight spades between them and are so weak they cannot even make a try for game. The points are probably fairly even and you and your partner almost certainly hold an eight-card fit, probably in clubs. You must bid 3C here.

It is very unlikely that either of your opponents can double you, and you will almost certainly not fail by more than two tricks. If your opponents bid on to 3S, leave them there: if they make it, you have lost nothing; if they go one down, you have scored a major coup.

South

♠ 94

♥ AJ43

♦ 986

♣ QJ103

N	E	S	W
–	1S	NB	2S
NB	NB	?	

Double for take-out. I know it won't be ideal if partner bids 3D, but he may well hold a five-card diamond suit. Even if you bid at the 3-level with a seven-card fit, your opponents probably won't realize this and they may still bid on.

Incidentally, opponents who agree a trump suit, particularly a major, are psychologically geared up to play the hand. They hate changing their mind and defending instead. So, people very often bid up – and that is what you want.

Next time you see an auction like this, where your opponents bid one–two and then stop, keep an eye on the player who thinks he, or she, is about to play the hand. They often sit up, adjust their bottoms on the chair – their entire body language indicates that they are in charge of this deal and they are going to play the hand and show you how wonderful they are. Take the opportunity to burst their balloon of pomposity – it will really annoy them.

On both occasions in the above examples, you held only an 8-count. However, you had the right shape for your bid. Whenever you enter the auction to exert pressure on your opponents, do not worry about points; just ensure that you have the correct distribution.

South

♠ 943

♥ AQ43

♦ A83

♣ QJ10

N	E	S	W
–	1S	NB	2S
NB	NB	?	

A better hand, but the wrong shape – well, no shape at all. But, should you still bid? I would say yes. Your opponents may, on rare occasions, have only a seven-card fit, but assuming that they have an eight-card fit, your partner has shape (a doubleton spade at least), but lacked the points to enter the auction. Double, and hope that you find an eight-card fit yourself. Letting your opponents play at the 2-level when they want to is a bad idea.

This last example is more for Duplicate Pairs players; in Rubber or Teams-of-Four Bridge, to pass is quite reasonable.

South

♠ 97
♥ A42
♦ 98
♣ KJ10983

N	E	S	W
–	–	–	1S
NB	2S	?	

This is quite different. This time, your opponents have not stopped in 2S, they are in the process of bidding which has so far reached 2S. Surely it can't be right to bid now?

Yes, it surely can. Bid 3C. If West is planning to pass 2S, then your partner may be unable to make a bid to push them up. This is because you have a decent hand and a shortage in spades, making it likely that your partner does not have a shortage in spades. Therefore, if you do not bid now, your side may end up defending 2S.

What, you may ask, will happen if West was planning to bid 4S? Well, he'll probably bid 4S anyway. You will have given away a little information but at least have attracted a decent lead. Is he likely to double you? As mentioned above, bridge players like playing hands, and if they are faced with a choice between defending a part-score and bidding game, they usually go for the latter.

What you actually hope will happen is that either you are left to play in 3C – maybe failing by one or two tricks – or that your opponents bid on to 3S and then go one down.

So, what we really come down to is this:

Once your opponents have agreed a suit, all your competitive bids become merely shape showing and not reliant on points at all.

Provided that you and your partner know this, little will go wrong, and you will earn a reputation for being very difficult to bid against.

This method is not a good idea when playing with a new

partner, and probably not necessary at Rubber Bridge or Teams-of-Four, but, for Duplicate Pairs, it is wonderfully aggressive, logical and effective.

When your opponents have not agreed a suit, your bids should be full strength and the correct shape.

And don't forget this bit either. It is sometimes hard to be disciplined but, when your opponents haven't found a fit (yet), that is the best way to be.

If one side has an eight-card fit, the other side will also have one and therefore both sides should be bidding.

When one side does not have an eight-card fit, neither will the other side. The hand is a misfit and you should be very wary of entering the auction.

Since both sides are inextricably linked, we can go even further:

If the hands are fitting, bid;
if the hands are not fitting, stay out of it.

Lead-directing doubles: positive and negative inferences

I advocate a simple system of low-level doubles against conventional bids:

- If you double a low-level conventional bid, this is lead-directional and suggesting five cards or more in the suit bid.
- If your right-hand opponent opens a game-forcing 2C, and you have five decent clubs or better, you can double to show this.
- If 2C is opened and the responder bids 2D, you can double to show a decent five-card diamond suit or longer.
- If an opponent responds 2C Stayman, a double shows five or more clubs; similarly with Transfers.

High-level doubles are often lead-directing also, but do not promise length in the suit. You might double a Blackwood response with KQ10 in the suit, as you know that this would be a safe – and attacking – lead; equally, you might double such a bid with a void.

There are more expert treatments, but this method has the advantage of being simple and easy to remember. Many top players double in these situations with only four good cards in the suit but, since you want to keep open the chance to compete in the bidding, I prefer to keep it to a five-card suit.

Be aware that if you double and your partner is not on

lead, you may have provided extra information for the declarer, but do not let that restrict you too much.

One of the best moments to double for a lead is when an opponent uses Fourth Suit Forcing and you want to ensure that partner makes that lead and not anything else.

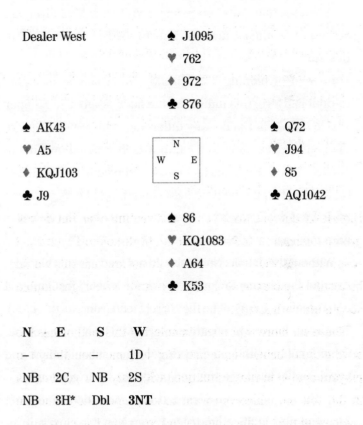

Dealer West

♠ J1095
♥ 762
♦ 972
♣ 876

♠ AK43
♥ A5
♦ KQJ103
♣ J9

♠ Q72
♥ J94
♦ 85
♣ AQ1042

♠ 86
♥ KQ1083
♦ A64
♣ K53

N	E	S	W
–	–	–	1D
NB	2C	NB	2S
NB	3H*	Dbl	3NT

When East used Fourth Suit Forcing, South decided that a

heart lead would surely be best and doubled to ensure that North chose that suit. West bid 3NT and, when North led 7♥, West found he had only one heart stopper and then, when he lost A♦, South cashed his heart winners; even the club finesse was wrong.

When partner asks you to lead a suit via a lead-directing double, it is almost always right to lead your top card in this suit.

Instead of bidding 3NT directly, West should probably re-double. Here, this indicates one hard stopper (a stopper where it does not make any difference whether West plays the hand or East plays the hand), which could allow East to bid 3NT if it was a superior contract played from his side of table – as it would be if he held something like ♥Q94. Even here, East declaring 3NT is superior, since North can never gain the lead.

Without the double, North should not lead a heart: his partner had the chance to double to ask for a heart lead and did not; therefore, it cannot be the correct lead from North's hand. This is an important negative inference which, once you become familiar with lead-directing doubles, should allow you to rule out at least one suit and pick from those remaining.

In the example above, even if East-West decide against 3NT and play in 4S, a heart lead from North is clearly best.

Doubles of Splinters

Many experienced players agree that a double of Splinter indicates interest in the suit above the one in which Splinter has occurred. However, having played this method for many years, I can report that it has never once come up. I therefore recommend playing that a double of Splinter indicates five or six good-quality cards in the suit bid, and suggests that if partner has four- or five-card support for that suit, he considers bidding on in this suit, prepared to fail in that contract rather than letting the opponents make theirs.

So, this double falls into line with all the others described above.

Doubles of 3NT

Doubles of 3NT are almost always lead-directing since it is most unlikely that your opponents have reached 3NT without sufficient values or a decent chance of using a long suit.

If there has been no opposition bidding, there are two key understandings to recognize:

N	E	S	W
–	–	1D	NB
1H	NB	1NT	NB
3NT	**Dbl**		

With West on lead, East has doubled to attract a specific lead. When your opponents have bid suits on the way to 3NT, this double asks West to lead dummy's first bid suit – here, hearts. Almost always, it is correct to lead the higher/highest card in this suit.

East may hold one of these hands:

(a)	(b)	(c)
♠ 965	♠ A3	♠ 743
♥ AQJ106	♥ KQJ106	♥ AKQJ9
♦ A53	♦ 832	♦ 732
♣ 86	♣ 962	♣ 105

In each case, a heart lead is likely to defeat 3NT whereas, without a heart lead, 3NT is very likely to make. Notice that, in each instance, the heart quality must be very high, in case dummy contains five poor hearts. Do not be surprised by example (c). Since the responder must show any four-card major suit in response, it happens that, sometimes, you hold solid cards in the suit. Without the heart lead – which your partner will not find without your double – the opponents will almost certainly succeed.

When the opponents do not bid any suits on their way to 3NT, the double has a different meaning:

N	E	S	W
–	–	1NT	NB
3NT	**Dbl**		

A double here asks West to lead his shorter major suit. The reasoning is that since your opponents have neither bid a major, nor employed Stayman, there is a chance that East-West could hold a strong major suit between them – or one of them may have a very strong suit. East might have:

	(a)	**(b)**	**(c)**
♠	KQJ104	J82	AKQJ10
♥	53	AQJ1093	J32
♦	A3	32	52
♣	J862	A2	108

Once again, the correct lead of West's shorter major should result in defeat for 3NT, whereas with a standard passive lead, 3NT was likely to succeed.

Many (many) years ago, the fearsome partner I was playing with made such a double and I did not lead my shorter major. You should have seen the blood rise to her face, her hands tremble, her eyes burn into me. With great difficulty, she said nothing – and neither did I. During the following hand, an opponent suddenly said: 'You didn't have any, did you?' – and my secret was revealed. If you have a long major it is just possible that your partner is ultra-short – and then there can be a temporary strain, to say the least, on partnership harmony . . .

If your partner doubles 3NT and you have bid a suit, or if he has bid a suit, then the double confirms that that is the suit to lead.

Others may agree differently but I believe that this is the easiest and most logical approach.

Whatever you decide, as long as you and your partner are in agreement, this will cut out the errors that damage your score so badly and affect your partnership confidence. In doing that, you will soon see your partnership grow.

Weak bids and strong bids – how to know which is which

A source of great frustration to partners over the years is working out the strength of a particular bid in a situation with which the partnership may not be familiar. Test yourself – and your partner – on these problems. If you both get them all correct, you are one class act.

1   Opponent opens 2C (game-forcing); partner overcalls 2S.

2   Opponent opens 2C (game-forcing); partner jump-overcalls to 3S.

3   Opponent opens 2S (weak); partner overcalls 3H.

4   Opponent opens 2H (weak); partner jump-overcalls 3S.

5   Opponent opens 1C, you pass, other opponent passes; your partner bids 2NT.

6   Opponent opens 2H (weak); partner overcalls 3H.

7   Opponent opens 1D, you pass, other opponent passes; partner jump-overcalls 2S.

8   You open 1H; opponent overcalls 1NT (16–18pts); partner bids 2D.

As we approach the answers, it is worth mentioning that mine are only the most commonly played methods. If you and your partner have a solid agreement as to the meaning of these bids, then that is just fine. However, I do strongly advise you to follow a key principle in bidding:

Over an opponent's strong bid, your bids will be weak;
Over an opponent's weak bid, your bids will be strong.

This principle will hold good 99 per cent of the time and should guide you towards the right answer when you are unsure of partner's strength.

1 Your opponent has opened the strongest bid available to him, and your partner's bid should be showing a weak hand, perhaps with five decent spades.

2 Once again, over your opponent's strong bid, partner's jump-overcall will be weak, regardless of your usual agreed strength for a jump-overcall. Non-vulnerable, partner will have a decent-quality six- or seven-card suit; vulnerable, a high-quality seven-card suit and some outside shape.

Non-vulnerable	Vulnerable
♠ KQJ852	♠ QJ98765
♥ 63	♥ 6
♦ J109	♦ QJ104
♣ 85	♣ 8

3 Over a Weak Two opening bid, all bids should be strong – to make a weak bid over a weak bid is almost always wrong. Even for a simple overcall, a robust opening hand with, ideally, a decent six-card suit is required. The reasoning behind this requirement for extra strength is that the pre-empt has warned you of poor distribution and if your other opponent holds four of your trumps, you want them at least to be four poor ones.

4   Whatever agreed strength of jump-overcalls you usually play, over a Weak Two opener, the jump-overcall should be played as strong. Here, you should expect partner to hold something approaching a Strong Two opener himself; with a six-card suit, seven to eight playing tricks.

5   How strong are your NT overcalls in the protective position? A 1NT overcall in the protective position conforms to most bids there and requires about 4pts less than a direct overcall, about 11–14pts, with one stopper or more in the opponent's suit. A jump-overcall to 2NT, however, is NOT the Unusual NT Overcall, but a natural strong bid, showing 19–21pts (you might widen the range a point each side), with one stopper or more in the opponent's suit.

6   How do you usually play your immediate cue-bid of the opponent's suit? Perhaps you play Michaels Cue-bids, or Ghestem? However, these two-suited overcalls can be relatively weak and generally it is wrong to apply them in these situations. Most experts would play 2H, 3H to show the following type of hand:

♠ K8
♥ 63
♦ AKQJ842
♣ A5

The bid says that you want to bid 3NT – almost always based on holding a strong hand with a long minor suit – but that you lack a stopper in the suit opened. If partner can provide a stopper, even something like ♥J1075, then he bids 3NT; if he cannot provide a stop, he bids 4C, allowing you to pass or correct to 4D.

This is the most logical use for the cue-bid over a Weak Two since, if your opponent holds a long major suit with few points, the chances that you hold a long minor suit with many points are increased.

7 As with answer 5, the jump-overcall in the protective position should always be strong and not your usual agreed strength. In the protective position, you have so many weak, and weaker, bids you can make, it is vital to preserve some to show a genuinely strong hand. All such jump-overcalls show hands not far off a Strong Two opener, with a high-quality six-card suit and something in the region of seven to eight playing tricks.

8 I include this example only because I so frequently notice that players do not seem to understand the position. When an opponent overcalls 1NT, showing 16–18pts, your partner has a simple choice: With 10pts or more (some people might play this with 9pts) you must double to indicate that your side holds the majority of the

points. At this stage, this is a penalty double. With fewer than 9/10pts, any change of suit shows a weak hand, usually with a long suit. Most players would play such a change of suit, even at the 2-level, as completely non-forcing and usually as intending to play there.

Partner opens 1H, opponent overcalls 1NT (16–18pts):

(a)	(b)
♠ K92	♠ 765
♥ 63	♥ 632
♦ K109	♦ 4
♣ AJ843	♣ KQJ843

(a) Double. Get the message across to your partner: we have the majority of the points.

(b) 2C. Non-forcing, usually to play.

Competitive bidding: before and after your opponents agree a suit

To succeed in the modern game you need to be aggressive and disruptive as often as possible. However, good players will be able identify positions where you have overstretched yourself and will opt to double you for penalties.

Overcalls at the 1-level can be modest in strength, and overcalling 1S is particularly desirable since, if your partner can raise you to 2S or even 3S, the barrage effect is maximized. However, to overcall at the 2-level is a much more serious option, and lays your side open to being doubled for penalties.

As you knew before, or know now, having read earlier:

If one side holds an eight-card fit, the other side will almost always hold an eight-card fit in another suit.

I spent several years playing bridge before anyone explained this to me explicitly. Once you understand that the entire deal is either a fit for both sides, or a misfit for both sides (there can be a few low-level exceptions where one side holds an eight-card fit and the other side holds three seven-card fits), the whole concept of competitive bidding begins to fall into place.

When you overcall at the 2-level before your opponents have agreed a suit, it is a strong manoeuvre, which risks good opponents doubling you for penalties. So, I urge you to respect a 2-level overcall in these positions or face the consequences.

At equal vulnerability, your right opponent opens 1S and you hold:

(a)	(b)	(c)
♠ Q43	♠ 2	♠ A76
♥ J53	♥ QJ643	♥ 32
♦ A3	♦ J832	♦ AKJ974
♣ AJ862	♣ AKQ	♣ 108

(a) Pass. This would be an awful overcall of 2C. It barely obstructs your opponents' auction, and your suit quality is poor.

(b) Pass. This is not suitable for an overcall of 2H, since your spade shortage is not an advantage (you will be trumping in your own hand) and your suit quality is poor. To double would risk missing a 5-3 heart fit or playing in an awkward 4-3 club fit.

(c) 2D. A good six-card suit. You are taking almost no risk by overcalling, attracting the right lead, and being mildly obstructive.

To overcall at the 2-level before your opponents have agreed a suit, you require an opening hand with a high-quality five-, or preferably six-card suit.

At equal vulnerability, your left-hand opponent opens 1S, partner passes and your right-hand opponent bids 2C:

(d)	(e)	(f)
♠ AJ3	♠ 2	♠ A7
♥ KJ753	♥ QJ64	♥ KQJ1097
♦ 73	♦ AQ832	♦ A4
♣ Q62	♣ KJ7	♣ 863

(d) Pass. Your opponents have opened and responded at the 2-level, so they clearly hold the majority of the points. They have not found a fit and, if they do not have one, neither will you. You gain nothing by bidding and risk losing a sizeable penalty when things go wrong. If your opponents end up playing the hand – as they are likely to do – you will have told them where the points lie and what your distribution might be. Finally, your values are poorly positioned – your J♠ and Q♣ are both useful defensively and are likely to be of little use playing the hand. In short: shut up!

(e) Pass. You have both unbid suits but competing now is a mistake. If your opponents show weakness and subside in 2S, you might double for take-out later. For now, since your opponents are likely to buy the contract, keep quiet.

(f) 2H. Lovely hand, pure values, six-card suit, no danger of being doubled, and, if your opponents have a fit, your partner might – just might – be able to support you.

I think what these last three examples actually illustrate is that when your opponents open the bidding and change the suit, especially at the 2-level, overcalling is a pretty poor idea unless you have a really good six-card suit and a strong hand . You may well get the chance to compete later – bidding now is likely only to help your opponents when they come to play the hand.

When your opponents open the bidding and change suit,

particularly if it is at the 2-level, be VERY reluctant to enter the auction even with a decent opening hand.

Here are two hands from recent play to show you just how important it is to consider the difference between overcalling after your opponents have agreed a suit (and therefore you know that the hand is fitting) and sticking your neck out when there is no evidence of a fit on the hand.

Dealer South

Love All

	♠ J984	
	♥ 72	
	♦ AQ62	
	♣ 1065	
♠ A107		♠ 2
♥ J96	N	♥ KQ1054
♦ J983	W E	♦ 1075
♣ Q73	S	♣ K984
	♠ KQ653	
	♥ A83	
	♦ K4	
	♣ AJ2	

N	E	S	W
–	–	1S	NB
2S	3H	?	

East certainly sticks his neck out by bidding 3H, but it does have many advantages, not least the eventual result on this deal. With North-South having agreed spades, East-West have an eight-card fit and hearts is the most likely spot. If South had been weaker and West a little stronger, South would have passed 2S and West would have been unable to protect, having no shape, and North-South would have got to play in an easy 2S.

As it is, North-South can bid 4S, and they may be able to get there if they are given space. South incorrectly bid 3S and North passed. North was correct since, to continue bidding your agreed suit in a competitive auction is always merely competitive and never a try for game.

To make a game try after this intervention, South should either introduce a new suit, even if it is only a three-card suit, or here, where there is no room to introduce a new suit, double. In this position – after intervention leaving no other bidding space – this is a 'game-try double', inviting partner to bid 3S if minimum for his original raise, or 4S if maximum, which is what South would like to imply.

Notice that at no time would North or South ever have considered doubling 3H for penalties. They have their own fit and are far more likely to bid on than to try to defend.

In a competitive auction, if you continue bidding your own side's suit, it is always non-forcing, usually indicating extra length in your suit but not extra values.

If you want to make a try for game, introduce a new suit or, if no room is available, double – these actions invite partner to go to game if he is maximum for his bidding so far, or to pass or correct to the agreed suit if he is minimum.

As discussed, to overcall, especially at the 2-level or above, when your opponents have not agreed a suit, promises solid values and a really high-quality suit. If the hand proves to be a misfit, then being doubled for penalties is a real danger. If your opponents do this and defeat you when there was no making contract for their side, you will have scored very badly.

Dealer North   ♠ Q7

Game All   ♥ AK972

                       ♦ K1052

                       ♣ 106

♠ J10		♠ A9842
♥ QJ6	N	♥ 1054
♦ AQJ983	W E	♦ 7
♣ 94	S	♣ QJ72

                   ♠ K653

                   ♥ 83

                   ♦ 64

                   ♣ AK853

N	E	S	W
1H	NB	2C*	2D
NB	NB	**Dbl**	

* 1S might be the better response.

This a classic example of poor overcalling. West, with a classy six-card suit, thought he would slip in a 'safe' overcall, but it ended in disaster. His ♥QJ and J♠ are likely to be useless and the overcall achieves nothing. 2D doubled might go three down, but even two down doubled is a dreadful result. North-South are very unlikely to make a game contract with their combined 22pts, and +500 will look great – for them – on the scorecard.

What can West's overcall gain? Almost certainly nothing. Diamonds will not buy the contract and certainly bidding 2D causes no disruption to his opponents' auction. If East-West end up defending, bidding has provided a blueprint for North and South to follow when they play the cards.

Await developments with shapely, but weak, hands

Your left-hand opponent opens 1H, partner passes and your right-hand opponent bids 1S. What will you bid on these hands?

	(a)		(b)		(c)
♠	75	♠	AQ98	♠	–
♥	3	♥	QJ64	♥	32
♦	QJ873	♦	A2	♦	AKJ97
♣	AJ862	♣	KJ5	♣	QJ10864

(a) Pass. You have the right shape for an Unusual NT Overcall – here 2NT – but your suit quality is poor, and your hand is weak. It is better to pass now and wait to see how strong your opponents are. If they subside in 2H or 2S, you can come in, knowing that your partner holds some values, and apply pressure by stealing the contract in 3C or 3D, or pushing your opponents to the 3-level.

If you bid and the opponents buy the contract – as they are likely to do – your bidding presents a great description of your hand from which they can make an accurate plan to bring home their contract.

(b) Pass. Many players would overcall 1NT here, but I would rather defend whatever contract my opponents find. The hand seems very much like a misfit, so defend. Why tip them off that the hand is going to go badly for them when they have to bid at least once more?

(c) 2NT. This time you have excellent quality and good strength, not to mention extra shape, and it is better to bid now so that if your opponents find a fit, and jump, your partner is primed for a sacrifice bid if he holds four- or five-card support for one of your suits.

As before, if your opponents agree a suit, you can enter the auction with a take-out double or Unusual NT overcall on much weaker hands but with the correct shape.

Free bid or forced bid?

There is one situation where the meaning of a seemingly modest little bid changes quite considerably and which, if not discussed, can sometimes lead to trouble.

What is the difference between these two auctions?

(a)					(b)			
N	E	S	W		N	E	S	W
1S	NB	1NT	1H		1H	S	1NT	

South's 1NT response in auction (a) should show 6–9pts, deny three-card support or better for spades, and could be completely unbalanced.

In auction (b), South's response shows 6–9pts, at least one solid stopper in spades, and promises two- or three-card support for partner's hearts.

This difference occurs because in auction (a), if South holds 6pts or more, he must bid something to allow North to rebid. In Acol-based systems, the 1NT response shows the weakest of hands and is used only to keep open the auction.

In auction (b), South no longer has to bid to keep open the bidding since East's intervention ensures that North will get a chance to rebid anyway. To bid on the South hand with a misfit – a singleton or void in North's heart suit – would be to encourage partner at quite the wrong time.

So, South's hand in auction (a) could be:

♠ –
♥ Q63
♦ J8754
♣ K7652

Whereas, in auction (b), South must hold at least two-card support for partner's suit to *freely* bid 1NT. (Please forgive the split infinitive.)

Incidentally, I think that it makes perfect sense for your 1NT response to 1H or 1S – in an uncontested auction – to deny three-card support. When the opener holds a five-card major suit, he knows that it is not correct to rebid it, unless the texture is perfect. Whilst you may end up playing in a 4-3 fit at the 2-level, further bidding of the agreed major after this auction requires the opener to hold five cards or more in the suit.

Equally, supporting with three cards is more pre-emptive than responding 1NT and clearly differentiates between the two actions.

The one time I might consider responding 1NT with three-card support for partner's hearts is on a hand such as this. Partner opens 1H and you hold:

♠ QJ9
♥ 632
♦ J94
♣ QJ85

Here, there is no chance of a ruff, all your values are no-trump orientated (see page 16) and your trump quality is very poor. 1NT certainly seems superior to bidding 2H here.

When you know what's happening, bid immediately to the right contract

This suggestion does not entitle you to guess the final contract because you can't be bothered to bid accurately, or because you do not know the convention. This is a tip to remind you that, as soon as you know what you need to know from an auction, just bid the correct contract.

Take this hand, which occurred recently in an event:

West	West	East
♠ AQ42	1C	1S
♥ 6	4S	4NT
♦ 7	5S	5NT
♣ AK98743	?	

You may or may not agree with the rebid raise to 4S, but whilst there are many options, none are great. However, when East starts using Roman Key-Card Blackwood (or indeed traditional Blackwood), it is pretty exciting. Surely partner has two aces and a spade suit headed by king-jack? When you show two key-cards plus the trump queen (or just two aces in ordinary Blackwood) and partner then asks you for kings, you know that he is looking for grand slam (you should only be asking for kings if you are

seeking the grand; otherwise, just bid a safe small slam).
What should you bid?

The answer is 7S. Partner cannot know the amazing shape
of your hand, and a seven-card suit headed by AK plays bril-
liantly opposite any holding. Partner may think you need to
hold a specific king to make the grand slam but you know
better, so bid what you know must be able to make.

The following hand came up in the final of an inter-club
event in London:

West	West	East
♠ AKQ4	1D	3D
♥ 6	3S	4C
♦ A975432	4S	4NT
♣ 7	?	

West's 3S may, at that point, have been be a Stopper-Showing Bid for no-trumps, merely showing a spade stopper.
However, when East cue-bids 4C (showing A♣) and West
then rebids 4S, he is now showing A♠ and K♠. East launch-
es into Roman Key-Card Blackwood. Normally, West would
reply 5H, showing two key-cards but no trump queen. However, since West holds a seven-card diamond suit (when he
might easily only have had four cards), West should probably respond 5S, indicating two key-cards and the trump
queen. If East holds it, he may be confused, but it might be

worth agreeing that if you have six cards or more in a suit for which partner has shown four-card support, you show the trump queen even if you do not hold it, since your length will obviate the need for it anyway.

In any case, if East can really launch into Blackwood after this auction, the chance that he has two aces and the trump king are very high, so a grand slam is always looking likely.

East held just A♥, A♣ and K♦ and the grand slam resulted in a big swing to the side who bid it.

Pre-emptive manoeuvres

Years ago, it would have been considered unfriendly, even unsporting, to make a pre-emptive bid. Opening with 3H or 3S was a very strong bid, reserved for very strong hands (which almost never appeared).

Even when people started supporting overcalls on very weak hands, some people were almost offended. (I got a long, angst-ridden email from a group of husbands whose wives had been taught aggressive overcall supporting by me, in which they claimed that this was tantamount to cheating and that I would get their wives into trouble! In the event, they just got a couple of lessons themselves and, all of a sudden, they didn't feel so bad any more.)

These days, at the highest level, ruining your opponents' auction, inhibiting even their first bid, is standard and desirable. In this section, we'll play around a little with the idea of a pre-empt and, just as importantly, discover the best way to defend against them when you face that challenge.

OPENING THIRD-IN-HAND

Particularly for Duplicate Pairs players, I am not a fan of light openers third-in-hand. To open at the 1-level on 9 or 10pts and a five-card suit simply because you feel it might be a little pre-emptive is generally not going to work for you. Good opponents will reach the right contract anyway and gain the advantage of knowing where the bulk of opposition points are located; your partner often finds himself unable to decide how strong you really are and to judge whether or not to compete.

All my experience tells me that, for the majority of the time, light 1-openers are a poor idea third-in-hand. (In fact, I think they are a pretty poor idea at any time, because they usually disturb your auction more than your opponents'.)

However, pre-emptive openers third-in-hand work very well. Having already seen partner pass, you have a new freedom to vary the strength – and length – of your pre-emptive openings, knowing that, having passed, all partner might do is support your suit to continue the barrage.

Whilst to open with a pre-empt in the first or second seat should require a certain – and agreed – suit quality, thus allowing your partner to judge what to bid should he hold a strong hand, in third position, you can relax.

As a general rule, when I open a pre-empt third-in-hand, I tell my partner that my point range is widened both up and down by several points and that my suit length may be one card fewer than usual. On this basis, partner will not support me without an extra card in my suit.

Third-in-hand pre-empts can vary in strength from weaker than usual to stronger, and they may contain one card less than usual (especially if non-vulnerable against vulnerable opponents). Partner should assume a shorter suit than usual and bid appropriately.

After two passes, and with both sides non-vulnerable, here are some examples:

(a)	(b)	(c)	(d)
♠ QJ9865	♠ KQJ987	♠ 64	♠ AQJ98
♥ 6	♥ 6	♥ A7	♥ 86
♦ 853	♦ 82	♦ AQJ732	♦ 62
♣ 632	♣ 9532	♣ 975	♣ 7432

(a) Your opponents definitely have a game contract and 3NT might be best for them. By opening 2S, you may make it harder for them to find that contract. At the very least, you are destroying two whole rounds of their bidding space.

(b) 3S. You have one card fewer than usual, but good quality, making the likelihood of being doubled for penalties much smaller. Furthermore, your opponents may well struggle to find their best spot.

(c) 3D. To open 1D strikes me as a mistake, since this deal is likely to be a part-score battle and your opponents are likely to have an eight-card fit in a major suit. By bidding 3D, you may buy the contract there and then or, if your partner is very weak, your opponents may chance 3NT and be dismayed to find that you hold an outside entry as well as your long suit. Your partner does not know whether you are a little weaker or stronger than your usual 5–9pts range for a pre-empt, but he should expect that you may be one card shorter.

(d) 2S. Another attempt to make your opponents work hard to find the right denomination and level, which might also mislead them a little if they play in 3NT and try to judge the layout of the hand.

Your convention card should declare that third-in-hand pre-emptive bids are more flexible in both point-count and suit length.

As with all competitive bidding, at the very least, partner should apply the Total Trumps Principle, bidding to the same number of tricks as you hold cards between you in your longest suit. In doing this, following a third-in-hand opening, he should place you with one card fewer than usual to ensure that a safe level is not passed.

When you are vulnerable, you must ensure that you do not offer your opponents an easy option of doubling you for penalties. Usually, when vulnerable, your pre-empt suit length should be standard, and the suit quality higher. However, when both sides are vulnerable, you must be prepared to take some risk in order to inhibit an easy auction for your opponents.

Defending pre-empts

Accurate bidding requires space to describe your hand and, as you will be all too aware, an opponent's pre-empt ruins your bidding sequence. Sometimes, pre-empts manage to keep the opponents out of the auction altogether. When they do find a bid, the partnership ends up guessing the best spot.

However, there are some useful rules to guide you into guessing correctly.

RESPONDING TO A TAKE-OUT DOUBLE OF A
3-LEVEL PRE-EMPT

I have included this example because it crops up so frequently and I still see almost everyone getting it wrong. Once a pre-empt has been made, this is a competitive auction and your trump length becomes key to surviving bad breaks and forcing defence.

This is the classic problem:

Dealer North	**West**
All vulnerable	♠ Q42
	♥ KJ86
	♦ A92
	♣ J73

N	E	S	W
3S	Dbl	NB	?

Partner is likely to have a robust opening hand with the correct shape. On average, I would say that you hold a wide range of 23–27pts between you and partner has a singleton spade.

Holding this hand, almost everyone bids 4H and, sometimes, it will make. But, as you have bid at the 10-trick level with only eight trumps, you are far from certain that you will make ten tricks, even if the trumps split 3-2. If they divide 4-1, as is quite likely after the pre-empt, you will struggle. You also have a likely spade trick in defence, but Q♠ will have no value playing in 4H. In short, 4H will make rarely and, when it does, 3S doubled will often go down three tricks for a penalty of +800, beating your +620 or +650. More importantly, when 4H goes one down, you will still be defeating 3S by one or two tricks, for +200 or +500. So, with this hand, at this vulnerability, the correct bid is to pass.

If your side is vulnerable and your opponents are not, it is a more close-run decision. I might well still pass, but I might also be tempted to try my luck in the eight-card fit.

Change the hand to this, and it becomes a straightforward bid of 4H.

West

♠ 942

♥ KJ863

♦ A92

♣ J7

Here, you have no defensive trick in spades, an extra trump of your own, and a little more shape. 4H is very likely to make now; 4S is likely to fail by less.

In a competitive auction, and especially over pre-empts, bid no more than one trick more than the number of trumps you and your partner hold between you.

STYLES OF HAND ON WHICH TO DOUBLE A PRE-EMPT

When you double a 1-opener, you traditionally show all three remaining suits, with a shortage in the suit opened. Very rarely, you might have a monster hand where you would have opened the equivalent of a Strong Two, or even a balanced hand with 19pts or more. You would never double on a two-suited hand, since you have, for example, the Unusual NT Overcall and Michaels Cue-bids (there are other excellent two-suited gadgets available).

After a pre-emptive bid, be it a Weak Two or a Weak Three, your double should show either all three remaining suits, or a stronger two-suited hand. With a strong single-suited hand, a normal overcall, or even a jump-overcall (depending on your system), will show that hand.

When you double on a three-suited hand, you will pass whichever suit your partner chooses, unless you are much stronger than he might expect.

With a two-suited hand, partner is likely to bid the suit you do not have (such is life with bridge partners) and you must bid the cheaper of your remaining two suits, so that your partner can pass or adjust to your other suit, ideally at the same level.

Here are some hands by way of example.

Your right-hand opponent opens 3D. What action do you take?

(a)	(b)	(c)	(d)
♠ KQ98	♠ K5	♠ AJ	♠ KQJ982
♥ AQ43	♥ KQJ874	♥ KJ953	♥ AKQ32
♦ 8	♦ 92	♦ 6	♦ 6
♣ A942	♣ AK3	♣ KQJ95	♣ 8

(a) A standard take-out double where, whichever suit your partner chooses, you will pass his response.

(b) A standard overcall of 3H. Since you never make a weak bid over a weak bid, your partner should interpret this as a strong overcall.

(c) Double. Your partner is likely to respond 3S, over which you will bid 4C, indicating a two-suited hand without spades. Partner can pass, correct to 4H or even consider bidding 5C.

(d) Double. When partner bids 4C, you must bid 4H, showing hearts and spades and allowing him to pass 4H or correct to 4S. If partner responds 5C, you should still bid 5H and the possibility of a 6H/6S contract is still in play.

The following deal cropped up in a crucial club match. One side reached the best contract:

Dealer West

```
              ♠ AK862
              ♥ AJ964
              ♦ 3
              ♣ A5

  ♠ 3                          ♠ J975
  ♥ 8          N               ♥ Q732
  ♦ J965    W     E            ♦ AQ7
  ♣ KQJ9842     S              ♣ 76

              ♠ Q104
              ♥ K105
              ♦ K10842
              ♣ 103
```

N	E	S	W
–	–	–	3C
Dbl	NB	3D	NB
3H	NB	**4H**	

When North rebid 3H, he showed a two-suited hand with hearts and spades. Despite holding only three-card support, South appreciated that his values were well placed – ♠Q10 and ♥K10 must all be useful cards, so he bid 4H.

Although it turns out not to be, even K♦ could have been working for North-South.

Notice that North did not get over-excited. His partner could have held fewer values and in less useful places. To rebid 3H was ample.

In this instance, South did not worry about only holding an eight-card trump fit. This is because he was sure that his side held a double fit – two eight-card fits or longer – and a double fit always produces extra tricks.

West led 3♠, which could have been brilliant but which usually, with a singleton trump, will not be. This sorted out the spade position for South, who could now play trumps from the top and make with some ease.

NO UNUSUAL NT OVERCALLS AFTER PRE-EMPTS

Unless you specifically agree, very strangely, to do so, there is no use of the Unusual NT Overcall after a pre-empt.

Assuming that your opponent opens with a Weak 2H (or, against hand d) a Weak 3H:

(a)	(b)	(c)	(d)
♠ AJ8	♠ 953	♠ AQ	♠ A2
♥ QJ8	♥ AQ	♥ 53	♥ K104
♦ AQJ97	♦ A5	♦ KJ6	♦ AKQJ4
♣ K2	♣ AKQJ63	♣ AKQJ95	♣ Q105

(a) Over an opponent's Weak Two opener, an overcall of 2NT traditionally shows 17–20pts, with one stopper or more in the opponent's suit.

(b) Over an opponent's Weak Two opener, an overcall of 3NT traditionally shows a hand with a long solid minor suit, with at least one stopper in the opponent's suit.

(c) Over an opponent's Weak Two opener, a cue-bid of the opponents' suit (say, 2H – 3H) shows that you believe you can make 3NT, but you have no stopper in the opponent's suit.

(d) Over an opponent's Weak Three opener, 3NT is to play, usually based on a hand with a long minor suit, but sometimes on just a flat 17/18pts+ where you feel you must bid something.

Once you have agreed a trump suit, you can't play with another suit as trumps

The purpose of this section is to remind you that, once you have agreed a suit, even a minor suit, you cannot subsequently end up playing with a different suit as trumps, although you may end up in a no-trump contract.

So, having agreed a suit, any new suits bid will be artificial. For example:

West	East
1H	3H
3S	

You have agreed hearts as trumps, so West's 3S bid must mean something else. Here, this would be a cue-bid, indicating A♠ and suggesting a hand too strong simply to bid game. When one player makes a cue-bid, he hopes that his partner will cooperate with cue-bids also, before using a variation of Blackwood and then bidding at the 5-, 6- or 7-level.

After a suit agreement, any new suit that is suggested at the 4-level or above is always a cue-bid (or, possibly, a Splinter) looking for a possible slam. With the exception of the example above – which is also a cue-bid – bids of new suits after suit agreement at the 2- or 3-levels are attempts to find a game contract. The most useful of these occurs after a minor-suit agreement.

Stopper-showing bids for no-trumps

These used to be called 'Minor Suit Trial Bids' but since that title is pretty meaningless, I have renamed them 'Stopper-showing Bids for No-Trumps'. This is because these are bids showing stoppers, looking for a no-trump contract.

Whenever you and your partner have agreed a minor suit, any new suit you bid at the 2- or 3-level is showing a stopper in the suit you are bidding, and asks partner to bid any suit he holds which contains a decent stopper. In this way, you can check that you have all the suits covered for a NT contract.

West		East
♠ AKJ		♠ 43
♥ 52	N	♥ KJ9
♦ KJ7	W E	♦ 10432
♣ AQJ54	S	♣ K962

West	East
1C	2C
2D	2H
3NT	

Having agreed clubs, West rebids 2D to indicate a stopper

in diamonds and a concern elsewhere. East bids 2H to show that he has a stopper in hearts. This is what West wants to hear, so he bids 3NT.

In order to start making Stopper-showing Bids for No-Trumps, the player initiating them must believe that his side has the points to make at least 2NT (23pts) or more. Stoppers are shown in the cheapest order available, and once all four suits are known to be covered, a player should go ahead and bid the NT contract.

West		East
♠ A2		♠ J43
♥ AQ853	N W E S	♥ 9
♦ 63		♦ AJ9
♣ K954		♣ AQ8732

West	East
1H	2C
3C	3D
3NT	

Here, the minor suit has been agreed later in the auction, but East's 3D bid is still stopper-showing. West bids 3NT as he has a spade stopper. He could bid 3S to allow East to play the hand but, for simplicity's sake, bidding no-trumps yourself once all four suits are covered is probably best.

West		East
♠ AJ432		♠ K5
♥ 74	N	♥ AJ93
♦ KQ65	W E	♦ AJ943
♣ K9	S	♣ 32

West	East
1S	2D
3D	3H
3NT	

With spades and diamonds having been bid, when East bids
3H, showing at least one stopper there, he must be worried
about the unbid suit, clubs. Here, West holds K♣ and that is
sufficient to bid 3NT.

West		East
♠ 2		♠ 843
♥ AK	N	♥ J3
♦ AQJ743	W E	♦ K965
♣ K954	S	♣ AQ87

West	East
1D	3D*
3H	4C
?	

* 10–12pts / eight losers

116

West rebids 3H to show a stopper in hearts and, when East bids 4C, he is telling West that he has no stopper in spades, but he does have one in clubs. This is very good news for West, not for a NT contract, but for a diamond slam. If East does not have values in spades, then all his points are where West wants them to be: in clubs and diamonds (and perhaps a little something in hearts.) West would be quite justified in bidding 6D directly here.

This last example shows how this gadget can be used to avoid bad no-trump contracts and find how well the hands are fitting with a view to a slam contract. If East had shown a spade stopper, it would have made a slam less likely (since you don't really want values opposite shortages for a slam). West would then decide whether to play in 3NT or 5D. However, when East showed nothing in spades, the hands fitted really well together for a diamond contract and the slam could be identified and bid.

Doubles

Double is the most flexible bid in the entire game and one experts utilize far more than social or club players. Comparatively rarely used as a mandatory penalty, doubles usually indicate values or, most often, a choice of suits in

117

which to play. Here are some uses for double which you and your partner may want to discuss, because these expert understandings allow for much partnership consultation and, although you don't really trust your partner (of course you don't), bridge is a game played best when both members of the partnership work together.

OVERCALL OR DOUBLE?

This is a little section to explain one of those prickly problems which comes up quite often.

What do you bid here?

West

♠ KJ5
♥ AJ984
♦ 2
♣ AJ73

N	E	S	W
–	–	1D	?

Do you double for take-out, or overcall 1H?

Not for the first time in bridge, a five-card major suit is going to take priority. With a take-out-double hand containing a five-card major, your first action should be to overcall your suit. This is so that, if your partner has three-card support or better, you can find your heart fit.

If the bidding continues without your partner showing heart support, you can double later:

West

♠ KJ5

♥ AJ984

♦ 2

♣ AJ73

N	E	S	W
–	–	1D	1H
2D	NB	NB	**Dbl**

Now, you have shown a take-out-double hand, including a five-card heart suit. Since North-South have got at least an eight-card fit in diamonds, your partner will have three little hearts (with three half-decent ones, he probably would have supported your overcall at the 2-level), a four-card club suit, or a five-card spade suit, and you can now locate your eight-card fit.

If you double first and then bid hearts later, that shows a completely different hand: something approaching a Strong

Two opener in hearts with a super-high-quality five- or six-card suit.

DOUBLE TO SHOW ONE REMAINING SUIT

Many of you may be familiar with this understanding but I wanted to mention it because I sometimes see terrible things happening in front of my very eyes. This is why us bridge teachers look so world-weary – we have seen the very worst of mankind . . .

West

♠ 52
♥ 84
♦ AKQ9
♣ AQJ92

N	E	S	W
–	–	–	1C
1S	NB	2H	**Dbl**

Why should you give up in the hand above when you have two lovely pure suits and your opponents may be about to stop at the 2-level? However, to bid 3D here would be reckless since, if partner prefers to play in clubs, he will then

have to bid at the 4-level. By doubling, you indicate a choice
of denominations, and that can only be diamonds and clubs.
Partner will chose between them, aware that you have more
clubs than diamonds in your hand, and that you are probably shaped 5-4, or possibly 6-5.

DOUBLE TO SHOW TWO REMAINING SUITS

Even more basic perhaps, but still worth a quick mention,
just to refresh your thinking:

West

♠ QJ52
♥ 4
♦ AJ9
♣ AQJ93

N	E	S	W
–	–	–	1C
1H	NB	2H	**Dbl**

You might bid 2S here, showing 5-4 in clubs and spades,
but it is better to double since partner could hold a weak
hand with five or six diamonds and no support for either
black suit. In these situations as East, I assume that my

partner is 5-4-3-1 and bid accordingly, although of course West could be 4-4-3-2 or even 4-4-4-1. Double is just so flexible and should be used regularly.

Incidentally, if you play negative doubles, in any style, it is your responsibility to reopen the bidding with take-out doubles as often as possible, since your partner's original pass may be because he is seeking to penalize your opponent.

VALUE-SHOWING DOUBLES

This section touches on a far more complex set of bids that is probably suitable only for more experienced players, yet, whenever I teach or play, these situations seem to occur so frequently and, without knowledge of these bids, you are put in a terribly difficult position. So, let's take a look at a 'Value-showing' Double:

West

♠ AJ2

♥ KQ106

♦ Q92

♣ A73

N	E	S	W
–	–	–	1H
NB	2C	2D	?

You open the bidding, your partner responds, and then your right-hand opponent overcalls. What can you bid here?

You can no longer rebid 2NT because you would be promising better cards in diamonds. Holding only one weak stopper could lead to disaster. Nothing else you might bid would describe your hand well.

The answer, in this situation, is to double. This shows that you were planning to rebid no-trumps but, because of the overcall, you can no longer do so. Your partner therefore knows that you have 15pts or more and probably one stopper in the opponent's suit.

Partner can now:

- bid no-trumps himself if he has a stopper in the opponent's suit;

- continue to describe the shape of his hand, just as he would have done over your NT rebid;
- pass your double if he feels the hands are mis-fitting, and go for a penalty.

In this way, you have turned your opponent's intervention into an opportunity to describe your hands even more accurately than if he hadn't overcalled. Obviously, judgement is still required, and you still may not find the best spot, but this simple bid gives you back some of your lost bidding space.

By the way, what would you bid on this hand?

West

♠ AJ2
♥ KQ1063
♦ Q92
♣ 73

N	E	S	W
–	–	–	1H
NB	2C	2D	?

There is only one sensible bid to make and that is . . . Pass. The only reason why you normally have to make a rebid is to allow your partner to bid again. When an opponent intervenes after your partner's response, with a minimum hand, just pass.

If you do bid 2H, you should have a hand like this:

West

♠ J2
♥ KQ10632
♦ K92
♣ A3

N	E	S	W
–	–	–	1H
NB	2C	2D	**2H**

It is a non-minimum hand with a six-card heart suit and, although it is only a small thing, some fit, or good tolerance, for your partner's suit.

This is just a tiny element, but it represents an understanding of why you bid and what that bid means to your partner. That is what good bidding is all about.

Bridge terms to avoid

Possibly the best session of bridge I have ever played was when I was called in at the last moment to play for a regional team in South Africa in the final of the National Teams. We played against the then South African International team and the match was neck and neck right up to the final set of eight hands. My partner and I had barely three minutes to discuss our system and we spent most of it on discards and signals, rather than on the minutiae of bidding. As a result, we both bid as straightforwardly as we could and signalled obviously and clearly. Such simple methods proved to work a treat and we returned a strong card throughout.

So often I meet players who have agreed complex systems and conventions, yet there are two terrible deficiencies: they are not necessarily logical within the context of the rest of the system, and they include words such as 'feature' and 'suitable'.

I know how dangerous such words and phrases can be because I wrote some years ago in my book, *Control the Bidding*, that a Transfer break should be made to show a 'working doubleton'. How much I have regretted those two innocent words . . .

For me, a working doubleton is one which is more useful as a ruffing value than for the high cards it may contain.

In the context of breaking a Transfer what I really mean is a doubleton that does not contain a queen. All I needed to write was that: a doubleton not containing a queen. Instead, I wrote something fancy and my students and readers have questioned what I meant for years since.

There are a couple of further words and phrases that should be used with great care.

When there is a long pause in the auction and eventually my opponents reach their contract, I often ask the partner of the player who paused what his partner was required to show with his bid. The answer is often: 'a feature'.

What a horrible term that is. What is a feature? Is it values, or shortage, or both? Does QJx cut the mustard or do I need Kxx or Axx? What about Kx or Qx or a singleton or doubleton?

If you and your partner know what a feature is, then by all means continue to use that term to describe what you seek but, for me, a 'feature' could mean all sorts of things and is generally an excuse not to define what is required.

It is much better to agree that you will show:

- a *shortage*: a singleton or void; singleton or doubleton;
- a *holding* that reduces losers in a suit from, say, three to two, or three to one – which might be shortage or high-card values;
- *values*, when you specify what the minimum and maximum holdings might be.

127

If you define what you are seeking more accurately, it may limit its use but at least when you hear your partner's response you will have learnt something useful.

Another phrase misused and misunderstood is 'suitable hand'. It's the sort of thing a dubious politician might say – meaningless but, in some way, transferring any future blame onto someone else. Take this example:

West

♠ KJ9842

♥ Q86

♦ A9

♣ 73

N	E	S	W
–	1NT	NB	2H
NB	2S	NB	3S
NB	?		

Your partner opens 1NT (12–14pts) and you Transfer with 2H, showing a five-card spade suit; partner merely completes the Transfer. You now raise to 3S to show a sixth spade and invite partner to bid 4S with a 'suitable hand'.

Less experienced players might consider that this is enquiring whether the opener is minimum or maximum, or whether the 1NT opener holds two- or three-card support for spades. In fact, here, it refers to whether or not the 1NT opener is a hand more suitable for no-trumps or more suitable to play in a trump contract. The latter would be a hand made up predominantly of aces and kings, rather than one consisting mainly of queens and jacks. So,

(a)	(b)
♠ Q52	♠ A65
♥ AK73	♥ KJ53
♦ KJ4	♦ Q42
♣ 852	♣ QJ2

If East holds hand (a) I would like him to bid on to 4S and, if East holds hand (b) I would like him to pass.

This definition of the suitability of hands for no-trumps and suit contracts is incredibly important and one often overlooked. A hand which, when first opened, may seem terribly weak may, in the light of subsequent bidding, become a strong hand. For example:

West

♠ A64

♥ AJ52

♦ A732

♣ 73

N	E	S	W
–	–	–	1NT
NB	2D	NB	?

This is a horrible 1NT opener – you have mainly aces and your intermediate cards are all very low. It is the kind of hand that makes non-Weak NT players cringe at the thought of opening.

However, when partner makes a 2D Transfer bid (showing a five-card heart suit or longer), this hand is transformed. To play with hearts as trumps, this hand boasts four-card heart support, three aces and a doubleton club ideal for making ruffs. If I held this West hand, I might bounce to 3H but probably I would break the Transfer by bidding 3C (showing four-card heart support, and a hand suitable for playing a trump contract, containing a doubleton club for making ruffs). As a result, we may be able to reach a thin game or a slim slam.

In simple terms, hands are good for playing in no-trumps

if they contain queens, jacks, tens and nines, and/or five- or six-card suits of good quality. When valuing a no-trump hand, it is traditional to add half a point for tens and a point for every card over four in a long, decent-quality suit. Hence,

(a)	**(b)**
♠ Q109	♠ Q10
♥ A7	♥ A103
♦ KQ1074	♦ Q42
♣ 108	♣ KQJ97

Hand (a) is a perfectly decent 12–14pts 1NT opener and hand (b) is too strong to open 1NT and should be described by opening 1C and then rebidding 1NT to show 15–16pts.

This attention to detail will reap huge benefits at all forms of the game, but especially at Duplicate Pairs.

Hands are good for suit contracts when they contain aces, kings, singletons and voids and, of course, a long suit is always a benefit, whether it is trumps or a side-suit.

Other terms to avoid when muttering under your breath include: 'Idiot', 'Beginner', 'Obvious' (I hate hearing that one), 'Never again' and 'lost the will to live'.

Amazingly, man management, or just common courtesy and politeness, are essential skills in successful bridge partnerships, just as they are in business and life in general. Please ask yourself if you need some extra practice in this area . . .

CHAPTER THREE

DECLARER PLAY

IT IS VERY DIFFICULT to learn the play of the cards from a book. A good teacher with set hands, a patient partner who can watch you play and comment constructively: these are the best ways of improving.

However, if you read through the selection of tips and guidelines which follow and, when you are unclear on something, lay out the hands on a table with a pack of cards and play them through, I guarantee that you will improve. Until you have seen examples of certain plays, you cannot hope to spot them at the table in a random deal. This is the point of many of the following ideas.

Secret entries

Watching many hands being played, it is surprising how often a series of similarly themed random deals suddenly appear.

Dealer East

```
                    ♠ 1096
                    ♥ 1032
                    ♦ A643
                    ♣ 1043
    ♠ KQ52                      ♠ A83
    ♥ 84           N            ♥ K9765
    ♦ J75        W   E          ♦ 98
    ♣ QJ92         S            ♣ 765
                    ♠ J74
                    ♥ AQJ
                    ♦ KQ102
                    ♣ AK8
```

N	E	S	W
–	NB	2NT	NB
3NT			

North's three tens seduce him into raising to 3NT, and West leads 2♠. Since declarer is about to lose four spade tricks, to make his contract he is going to need the heart finesse to be correct. One successful finesse, however, is unlikely to be sufficient, so is there any way South can reach dummy twice to repeat the heart finesse?

At the table, declarer played K♦, then 2♦ to dummy's A♦, and took the heart finesse but, unable to return to the North hand, that was the end of the contract. With four diamonds in each hand, if the suits divides, it should be possible to get over to dummy a second time, providing you pay careful attention to the details. Incidentally, if the diamonds split badly, there is just too much to do.

Finally winning trick five after the four spade tricks have been lost, South should cash K♦ and Q♦, before crossing to dummy's A♦ by leading 10♦ from hand. He can now take the heart finesse. When that works, he leads his carefully preserved 2♦ over to dummy's 6♦, repeats the successful finesse, and claims his contract.

At another table, moments later, this hand crops up:

Dealer West

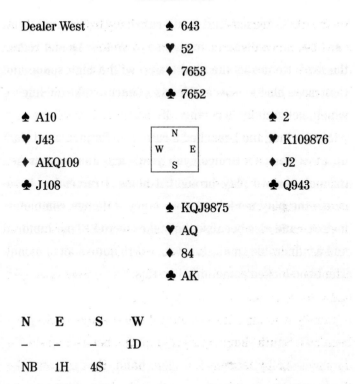

	♠ 643	
	♥ 52	
	♦ 7653	
	♣ 7652	

♠ A10
♥ J43
♦ AKQ109
♣ J108

♠ 2
♥ K109876
♦ J2
♣ Q943

♠ KQJ9875
♥ AQ
♦ 84
♣ AK

N	E	S	W
–	–	–	1D
NB	1H	4S	

West led A♦ and immediately declarer can see that to succeed, he will need to take the heart finesse and there appears to be no entry to dummy. However, with ten trumps between him and his partner, as long as they split 2-1, he should be able to reach the dummy hand by playing 5♠ to 6♠.

So, ♦AKQ are led, and South ruffs the third round – with 7♠! Now, he can lead trumps, lose to West's A♠ and regain the lead. He draws the final trump with a high spade and then plays his 5♠ to 6♠, and leads a heart to take the finesse which, delightfully, is correct. 4S made.

My partner and I reached a rather undistinguished slam up at St James's Bridge Club years ago and my partner, through shrewd play, brought it home. I remember it because the play made was very fancy – though completely logical – and also because the stakes were £10 per hundred and a vulnerable small slam was worth quite a lot of money. The hand looked something like this:

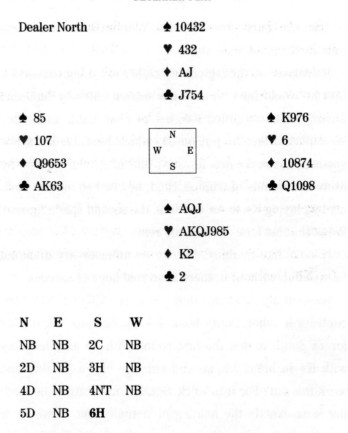

Dealer North

♠ 10432
♥ 432
♦ AJ
♣ J754

♠ 85
♥ 107
♦ Q9653
♣ AK63

♠ K976
♥ 6
♦ 10874
♣ Q1098

♠ AQJ
♥ AKQJ985
♦ K2
♣ 2

N	E	S	W
NB	NB	2C	NB
2D	NB	3H	NB
4D	NB	4NT	NB
5D	NB	**6H**	

2C was game-forcing and opener's jump-rebid to 3H set the suit. North's 4D was a cue-bid showing A♦. 4NT was ordinary Blackwood so, missing one ace, South settled for the small slam.

West led A♣ and, immediately, declarer can see that, unless East holds a singleton or doubleton K♠, he will need to take the spade finesse twice. With only one entry into dummy, how can he do that?

He arrived at the logical but rather shocking conclusion that he would have to create a second entry by finessing dummy's J♦. He ruffed K♣, led 2♦ from hand and, when West played low, he put on J♦, which held. He led a low spade and took the first finesse which also held, and now he drew two rounds of trumps. Next, he crossed over to dummy by playing K♦ to A♦ and took the second spade finesse. When that held, he claimed the rest.

It looks like madness to take an unnecessary diamond finesse but, without it, there is no real hope of success.

Incidentally, West can show amazing skill and defeat the contract if, when South leads his 2♦, he inserts Q♦. This forces South to win the first round with A♦ and, left only with K♦ in hand, his second entry is blown. Could West work this out? For it to work, South would have to be leading from exactly the holding he actually has. However, it is unlikely that Q♦ will have any value in the hand, since South almost certainly does not hold four diamonds so, perhaps, an expert West could and should find the defence.

Even when the entries are in plain view, players sometimes still miss them – or they start playing before realizing how vital a coherent plan will prove to be:

Dealer South

		♠ K63	
		♥ A865	
		♦ K2	
		♣ K843	

♠ Q1084			♠ J97
♥ 73	N		♥ K2
♦ A1076	W E		♦ 9854
♣ J92	S		♣ A1065

		♠ A52	
		♥ QJ1094	
		♦ QJ3	
		♣ Q7	

N	E	S	W
–	–	1H	NB
3NT†	NB	4H	

† Pudding Raise (showing four-card support, balanced hand, 13–15pts)

West leads 4♠ and South sees that there is a potential loser in each suit. However, holding ♦QJ3 in one hand and ♦K2 in the other means that a spade discard can be established and this must be done immediately. If you try to draw trumps and East wins (as he will), he will return a spade and open up your loser there before you have had time to deal with it. The standard rule in these situations is:

Preserve entries into the hand which contains the long suit you plan to establish.

To this end, you must win the first trick with K♠ in dummy, play K♦ and then 2♦ to your J♦, probably losing to West's A♦. When a second spade is led, you can win in hand with A♠ and play Q♦, pitching a spade from dummy. Now, when you lead Q♥ and run it, losing to East's K♥, East-West have no spade winner to cash. Win the spades the other way around and you have no fast re-entry to your hand and you will not be permitted to succeed.

When to rise and when to play low

This is not, I regret, advice that will provide the perfect answer to all your problems, but it will, I hope, help in a frequently occurring and often mis-played situation.

These examples mainly concern no-trump play, but there are occasions when such thinking is right in a suit contract also.

I am using diamonds as the suit only because it is the only one of the suit symbols which, when I try to draw it on a blackboard for my students, doesn't look like some kind of misshapen fruit.

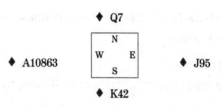

♦ Q7

♦ A10863

♦ J95

♦ K42

West leads 6♦ against South's 3NT contract. Should declarer rise with dummy's Q♦ or play low?

If dummy plays low, the diamond queen will be sitting there naked and exposed for all to see, and whoever holds A♦ will save it until they can slap it on top of Q♦. Your one hope of scoring the queen is to play it immediately. If it holds the trick, you still have K♦ in hand as a second stopper; if it loses, you can then hold up the king in hand until you believe that East is exhausted of diamonds.

This would be the same if dummy had ♦Kx and declarer ♦Qxx, but if dummy had three cards and declarer only two, then you would play low at trick one and try to score your doubleton honour in hand.

This situation has exceptions, but they are rare.

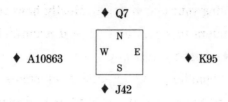

♦ Q7

♦ A10863

♦ K95

♦ J42

In this example, you have the jack and queen, and the difference is marked. Whereas in the first example, you had one certain trick and then a stopper with the chance of scoring a second trick, here, your aim is to ensure one trick.

If you rise with Q♦ this time, East will win with K♦ and return 9♦ and your ♦J4 in hand will be gobbled up by West's ♦A10. To ensure one trick, you must therefore play low from dummy. East must play K♦ to win the trick and now you still have both J♦ and Q♦ to guard against West's ♦A10.

These are simple understandings well known by good players, but if you are not familiar with them, just run through them again, laying out the cards on a table if necessary. They come up all the time.

Watch opponents' signals and discards

As mentioned in the defence section later in this book, there will be times when, as defenders, it is correct to false-card (play a card not normally considered the correct one, with a view to fooling your opponent[s]). Mostly, however, it will benefit defenders to signal and discard accurately since, nearly always, honesty does pay.

However, signalling your intentions, or shape, to your partner can be used against you, and alert declarers will use this information to boost their chances. This hand came up in one of my classes just the other day:

Dealer South

	♠ AQ1052	
	♥ Q7	
	♦ Q102	
	♣ K103	

♠ 973		♠ K8
♥ K52	N	♥ 10983
♦ 96	W E	♦ K543
♣ A9752	S	♣ 864

	♠ J64	
	♥ AJ64	
	♦ AJ87	
	♣ QJ	

N	E	S	W
–	–	1NT	NB
2H	NB	2S	NB
3NT			

Following a Transfer sequence from North, showing his five-card spade suit, South decided to pass 3NT, reasoning that his values – queens and jacks – were more no-trump orientated.

West led 5♣, which South won in hand. He led J♠ for the finesse, which East won with K♠ before returning his 6♣ which West won. West then cleared the suit by playing 9♣.

At this stage, South has eight tricks and must still tackle a red suit, but which finesse should he risk? If he gets it wrong, West will win and cash his club winners. Declarer correctly started to play out his spades and, on the third round, East discarded a heart, continuing with two more hearts on dummy's fourth and fifth spades. West discarded a heart and a diamond.

At this stage, declarer should have a good idea which red-suit finesse to take. When clearing a suit in no-trumps (pushing out the last high card from your opponent's hand) it is traditional to use a Suit-preference signal to indicate where your re-entry lies (see page 241). West chose to clear the club suit with his highest club, suggesting an entry in the higher-ranking suit: hearts, as opposed to diamonds. Then, East threw three hearts, suggesting he does not hold K♥. For these reasons, South should take the diamond finesse and, when it holds, his contract is secured.

As a general rule, opponents either discard the suit in

which they are least interested, or signal (usually with a high card) for the suit which they do want led. In each case, such information should benefit you, the declarer.

A favourite discard is the so-called 'spare fifth' – the fifth card in a suit a defender is not protecting because of its length. Whatever honour or honours the defender holds in this five-card suit, he can almost always afford to throw away one of the little cards.

When protecting a jack, the defender must retain three small cards to throw under the ace, king and queen (Jxxx).

To protect a queen, a defender needs two small cards (Qxx).

To protect a king, a defender needs only one small card (Kx).

And to protect an ace, a defender needs no small card.

So, assuming that a discard does not impart a specific message, it is easier for a defender protecting a king to throw away little cards in that suit than if he was trying to protect a jack.

Often a declarer is missing both an ace and a queen in a suit. If you were to play out your long trumps, it is more likely that the hand holding the ace would be able to throw away little cards in that suit, whereas the hand protecting the queen would have to hang on to at least two small cards to protect the queen.

Analyse opponent's lead

At the end of trick one, when most people pause to make their plan (it should be before touching dummy after the lead), I often ask my students which card was led. Sadly, all too often, the declarer has not paid any attention to it and cannot remember. The opponent's lead can be most revealing. While the leader is considering his options, I am reviewing the bidding and considering what I think is the most likely lead. If the opponent leads something I have not considered, then it is likely to be something a little unusual, such as a singleton.

This deal should be a reasonably simple declarer problem, but a failure to analyse the lead led to defeat.

Dealer South

```
            ♠ 5
            ♥ J96543
            ♦ Q10
            ♣ AQ75
```

```
♠ Q109432                    ♠ 876
♥ 102          N             ♥ A
♦ 2         W     E          ♦ K876543
♣ J432         S             ♣ 109
```

```
            ♠ AKJ
            ♥ KQ87
            ♦ AJ9
            ♣ K86
```

N	E	S	W
–	–	2NT	NB
3D	NB	4H	NB
4NT	NB	5S	NB
6H			

Over South's 2NT opening, North employed a Transfer to hearts and South bounced to 4H to show good-quality four-card support and a hand consisting mainly of aces and kings – suitable for playing with hearts as trumps. North pushed on with Roman Key-Card Blackwood, South showed two key-cards plus the trump queen, and North bid 6H.

West led 2♦ and South rose with dummy's Q♦ and beat

East's K♦ with his ace. He gave no thought to the lead, and instead laid down K♥. East won, returned a diamond, and West ruffed. One down.

Could South have known?

When an opponent leads a low card, it is usually from a three-card suit or longer headed by an honour or broken honours. To lead low from three or four small cards is usually quite wrong. A top-of-rubbish lead guides partner not to return this suit automatically. When East covers Q♦ with K♦, declarer should re-assess his initial thoughts. West cannot hold an honour card, not even the ten, and therefore the lead could well be a singleton.

To prevent defeat, declarer should play a spade at trick two, cashing A♠ and K♠, throwing away 10♦ from dummy. Now, when East wins the first trump lead and returns a diamond, dummy has none left.

One further consideration: if West's lead is a singleton, he might well hold 10♥. If he does, it will be necessary to retain J♥ in dummy to over-ruff this card. So, having pitched 10♦ on a top spade, declarer should lead K♥ from hand (not play low to dummy's J♥). Now, if East still returns a diamond, dummy can over-ruff West.

This situation, in 3NT, occurs more frequently than you might think. Once again, analysis of the lead at trick one is make or break.

Dealer South

♠ Q42
♥ 542
♦ A3
♣ KQJ85

7♦ led

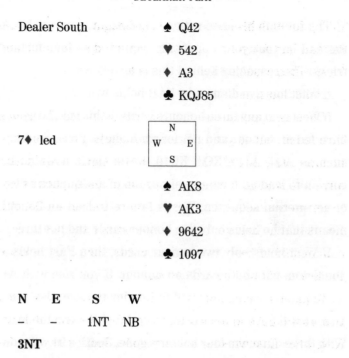

♠ AK8
♥ AK3
♦ 9642
♣ 1097

N	E	S	W
–	–	1NT	NB
3NT			

South finds himself in 3NT and West leads 7♦. Plan the play.

West's lead appears to be fourth highest of a suit – meaning four or five cards headed by an honour or broken honours. If West holds only four diamonds, your contract is safe since East-West can take no more than three diamond tricks and A♣. If West holds a five-card suit, however, you may lose five tricks.

Should you rise with A♦ immediately or play low, ducking a round?

The solution is to rise with A♦. In doing so, you will block the suit so that your opponents cannot cash four further tricks. The reasoning behind this is as follows:

If West has five diamonds, East holds two.

If West held any three honours cards in this suit, he would have led an honour and not fourth highest. From holdings such as AQJ, AJ10, KQJ, KQ10, KJ10, QJ10, it would be correct to lead an honour – either top of a sequence or top of an internal sequence. West's failure to lead an honour means that he holds only two honour cards and not three.

If West holds only two honour cards, then East holds a doubleton, with both cards an honour. If you rise with A♦ immediately, one honour will fall under the ace; the other honour will have to be overtaken by West to keep the lead. With three out of the four honours gone, South's 9♦ will now provide a fourth-round stopper.

Here is the full layout:

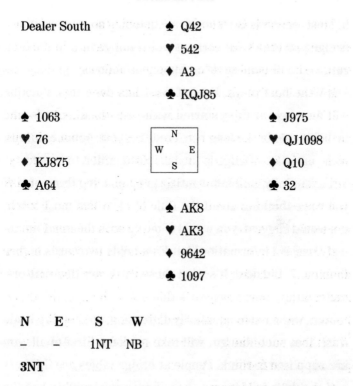

Dealer South

♠ Q42
♥ 542
♦ A3
♣ KQJ85

♠ 1063
♥ 76
♦ KJ875
♣ A64

♠ J975
♥ QJ1098
♦ Q10
♣ 32

♠ AK8
♥ AK3
♦ 9642
♣ 1097

N	E	S	W
–	–	1NT	NB
3NT			

If South ducks the first trick, East wins with Q♦ and returns 10♦ to dummy's A♦. When West wins A♣, he then cashes three more diamond tricks. Watch what happens when declarer rises with A♦ at trick one. Either East discards Q♦ to avoid the block (and later East's 10♦ falls under West's K♦), or East plays 10♦ at trick one and leaves himself with the bare Q♦.

You may argue that perhaps West has simply led fourth

highest because he knows no better. This is possible –
bridge players do all sorts of weird things but, in the long
run, you will beat such an opponent because he does not
know the best plays. Even if West has done this, ducking
will only help if East started with just two diamonds and
he holds A♣. In the long run, crediting your opponents with
some basic knowledge is the best assumption to make.

Incidentally, and not wanting to make a big thing of it, if
you were thinking about the Rule of 11, which most teachers would suggest, you would come up with the mind-numbingly useless information that East holds two cards higher
than the 7. Big deal. It's what those cards are that matters,
and a little thought can work that out.

And, while I'm momentarily digressing, don't worry if you
think that such thought will take too long. First of all, you
are supposed to think. People at bridge tables are thinkers
and should expect there to be pauses occasionally when the
declarer or defenders are working out what to do. Secondly,
the more you practise, the quicker you will become. And,
once you are used to the thoughts discussed above, you will
have room for others – and that's how you improve.

Assume that the lead against a NT contract is from a five-card suit

The reason why I like this assumption is that it is correct, or as correct as it needs to be, at least 95 per cent of the time and usually more. Importantly, it is guidance which will get you thinking in exactly the right way, allowing you to consider much more exciting and important matters, leading you to succeed in contracts which others might find complicated.

If your opponent has led from a four-card suit, often this is not a long enough suit to threaten your contract, and if he has led from a six-card suit, your assumption that it is a five-card suit, and the actions you take accordingly, will protect you sufficiently.

Let's start with something very easy to illustrate this thinking:

Dealer South

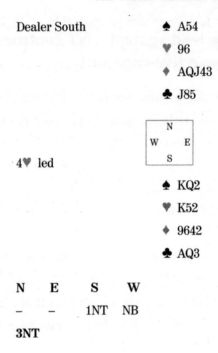

♠ A54
♥ 96
♦ AQJ43
♣ J85

4♥ led

♠ KQ2
♥ K52
♦ 9642
♣ AQ3

N	E	S	W
–	–	1NT	NB
3NT			

North correctly raises 1NT to 3NT, courtesy of his five-card diamond suit for which he should be counting an extra point. West leads 4♥. Instead of applying the Rule of 7 (by far the best of the rules out there), or the Rule of 11, just assume that West holds a five-card heart suit and count out the hearts in all four hands. West has five; dummy two, you have three and, therefore, East holds three hearts.

Your plan is to tackle the diamond suit, taking the finesse into the East hand. When you do this, you would prefer for

East not to hold any further hearts so that, if he wins, he cannot return a heart.

When East wins trick one with A♥ and returns 10♥, you know that East holds a third heart, so you duck this trick and West ducks also. East now leads 8♥ and you win with K♥.

If East has a heart left (and he has certainly played as if he does not), then the heart suit is 4-4 and you need not worry. As it is, you take the diamond finesse into the East hand and you do not care much whether it wins or fails. East has no hearts left to lead and you control the other suits.

This is an absolutely standard hold-up play, with a finesse into the 'safe' hand – the hand which does not hold any more cards in the danger suit (hearts).

Let's look at these hands:

Dealer South   ♠ 854
                          ♥ 54
                          ♦ AQ8
                          ♣ KQJ85

6♠ led

                          ♠ KJ3
                          ♥ A63
                          ♦ KJ64
                          ♣ 1097

N	E	S	W
–	–	1NT	NB
3NT			

West leads 6♠; East wins with A♠ and returns 9♠. What do you do?

You count out the spade suit, assuming that West holds five of them. This leaves East with just two spades. You must win the spade return with K♠ now since, if you do not, West is likely to switch to a heart and then you will lose a spade, three hearts and A♣.

This is the full deal.

Dealer South

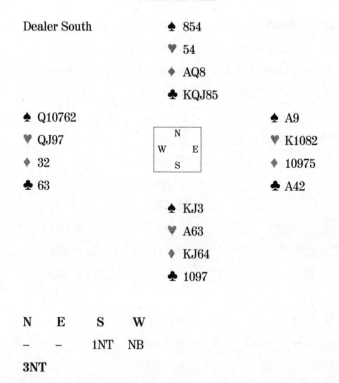

♠ 854
♥ 54
♦ AQ8
♣ KQJ85

♠ Q10762
♥ QJ97
♦ 32
♣ 63

N
W E
S

♠ A9
♥ K1082
♦ 10975
♣ A42

♠ KJ3
♥ A63
♦ KJ64
♣ 1097

N	E	S	W
–	–	1NT	NB
3NT			

If West is allowed to win trick two with Q♠, he should switch because he knows that South holds K♠ and, since he has no outside entry with which to regain the lead, he must look elsewhere for defensive tricks – a heart lead is safe and could (in this case, will) cause big trouble for South.

The advantage of assuming that West holds a five-card spade suit here is that it forces you to count out the hand, something which all good players do whenever they are trying to form a picture of their opponents' hands.

Such thoughts can help you to tackle hands where there seems to be a difficult decision:

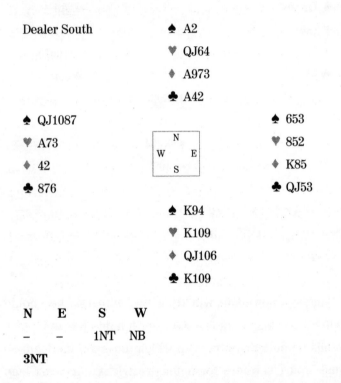

Dealer South

♠ A2
♥ QJ64
♦ A973
♣ A42

♠ QJ1087
♥ A73
♦ 42
♣ 876

N
W   E
S

♠ 653
♥ 852
♦ K85
♣ QJ53

♠ K94
♥ K109
♦ QJ106
♣ K109

N	E	S	W
–	–	1NT	NB
3NT			

West leads Q♠ and you, as South, must plan your play. You have two spades and two club tricks – you will need extra tricks from both hearts and diamonds. Which suit should you attack first?

The first thing to appreciate is that either player could hold A♥, but you can only lose K♦ to East. If West holds that card, you can finesse his king by leading Q♦ from hand and playing low from dummy every time he does not cover.

The next consideration is that, if you assume that West has led a five-card suit, then East is marked with three spades. This information combined will provide the solution.

Duck the first trick and win the continuation perforce with dummy's A♠. Now, play out hearts until the ace appears. West wins and leads a third spade which you now have to win in hand. Because three rounds of spades have now been played, you expect East no longer to hold any. When you finesse for K♦, East holds it and wins the trick. If he had a spade, the suit would probably be splitting 4-4 and you would still make your contract but, as it happens, he has none left and you make the rest of the tricks.

Again, thinking about the layout of the spade suit will help you to visualize the best way to make your contract.

When your opponent makes an opening lead of the lowest card out, this usually indicates that he holds four of them (as we make fourth-highest leads). However, this can be, on occasion, a perfect time for a false-card lead (see page 211) so, even then, it is nearly always correct to stick to the five-card rule.

At Duplicate Pairs, you may have to risk contracts in order to go for what you believe is the best chance of overtricks but, at Rubber, Chicago and Teams, safeguarding your contract should be paramount.

Look at this deal:

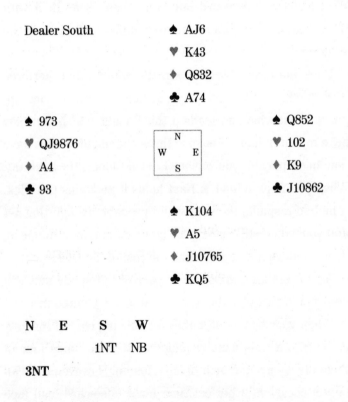

Dealer South

		♠ AJ6	
		♥ K43	
		♦ Q832	
		♣ A74	

♠ 973	♠ Q852
♥ QJ9876	♥ 102
♦ A4	♦ K9
♣ 93	♣ J10862

		♠ K104	
		♥ A5	
		♦ J10765	
		♣ KQ5	

N	E	S	W
–	–	1NT	NB
3NT			

West leads Q♥ and you, as South, decide what your best line of play might be. Even if you guess the position of Q♠, you are going to need at least one diamond trick. Your problem is that East-West will win their top diamonds, clear the heart suit, and still have time to cash their heart winners. What chances do you have?

East might hold three hearts and both A♦ and K♦, or West might hold a six-card suit, leaving East with just two hearts, in which case holding up the first round of hearts will exhaust East of that suit and sever communications. Assuming that West has six hearts and East only two is the layout that provides the best chance.

If South ducks trick one, West will continue with hearts and South wins in hand. When declarer now plays a diamond, East can win, but he has no hearts to lead. The contract is secure.

So, here, the assumption that West started with five hearts is not correct but, even so, the play of ducking the first trick is still correct, since what is appropriate for a five-card suit in the opponent's hand is usually right for a six-card suit also.

The point about these principles is that they stand you in good stead for most hands and, because they are understandings rather than just parrot-fashion rules, they help you to think about the exceptions, allowing you to develop winning lines of play.

Pay attention to the auction throughout the hand

If your opponents open the bidding, double or overcall, they may make finding the best contract harder for your side but, if you end up playing the hand, their actions have provided you with vital extra information on which to base your plan of attack.

It is essential to concentrate on your opponents' actions during the auction and throughout the play of the cards. Sometimes, the information provided can transform the hand for you.

Dealer West

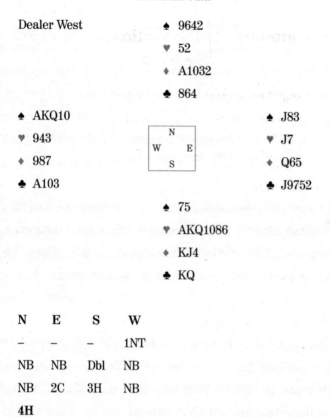

♠	9642
♥	52
♦	A1032
♣	864

♠ AKQ10		♠ J83
♥ 943		♥ J7
♦ 987		♦ Q65
♣ A103		♣ J9752

♠	75
♥	AKQ1086
♦	KJ4
♣	KQ

N	E	S	W
–	–	–	1NT
NB	NB	Dbl	NB
NB	2C	3H	NB
4H			

If E/W were non-vulnerable, South might punt 4H initially
but, with your opponents vulnerable, aiming for a big
penalty is the best initial action. East's 2C bid is now not
Stayman; most players cancel all conventions after an
intervention over 1NT.

West leads A♠ and South counts two spade losers, A♣

and a guess in diamonds as to who holds the queen. At the moment, it is more likely to be West since he has opened 1NT but, as always with two-way finesses, this decision should be left to the last possible moment.

Leave a finesse where you can pick up your opponents' queen in either hand, until the last possible moment.

West may continue with spades, laying down K♠ and then Q♠, which South trumps. Declarer draws three rounds of trumps. What should he do next? Since he has to lose A♣, this is a good moment to do it. He leads K♣ from hand; West probably wins with A♣ and leads 10♠. The hand is over now: you know who holds Q♦.

West opened 1NT and has shown up with ♠AKQ and A♣ – that is 13pts. He cannot hold Q♦ as this would mark him with 15pts. Of course, West may have mis-sorted his hand or deliberately opened 1NT with the wrong count but, almost always, he will have exactly 12–14pts. So, declarer leads 4♦ to dummy's A♦ and then 2♦; when East follows low, South puts on J♦ and this holds the trick. Contract made.

Two key elements here:

- you remember that West's bid promises 12–14pts and you count out the points with which he shows up;

- a two-way finesse – one which could be taken in either direction depending upon where you place the missing card – should be left until the last possible moment. Amass as much information as you can before committing yourself to that crucial play.

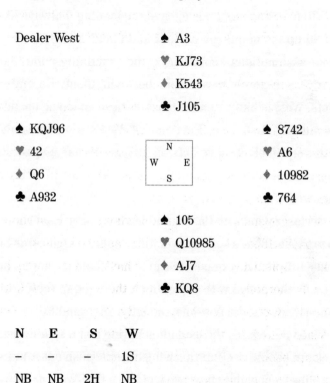

Dealer West

	♠ A3	
	♥ KJ73	
	♦ K543	
	♣ J105	

♠ KQJ96		♠ 8742
♥ 42	N	♥ A6
♦ Q6	W E	♦ 10982
♣ A932	S	♣ 764

	♠ 105	
	♥ Q10985	
	♦ AJ7	
	♣ KQ8	

N	E	S	W
–	–	–	1S
NB	NB	2H	NB
2S	NB	**4H**	

When South overcalls 2H in the protective position, North makes an Unassuming Cue-bid (UCB) to indicate an opening hand with heart support for partner. For more on what bidding an opponent's suit means, see page 60.

West leads K♠. Plan the play.

When an opponent has opened the bidding, I always like to add up the points my partner and I hold, and then make some assumptions about where the remaining points lie. Here North-South have 24pts between them; East-West 16pts. West is likely to have most of these, since he opened the bidding. Also, since East passed West's 1S opening bid, he is very likely to have 5pts or less. South has a spade, a heart and a club to lose and he will need to avoid losing a trick to Q♦.

Declarer wins with the A♠ and leads trumps; East shows up with A♥. That's 4pts and very likely all the high cards he holds. It is virtually impossible for him to hold Q♦ now; if he does, West opened with 10pts and East failed to reply with 6pts – the former is possible; the latter improbable.

When he regains the lead after having lost a spade trick, declarer should continue drawing trumps, push out A♣ and continue to play out clubs. He will learn that West held two trumps, almost certainly five spades (since East would have supported 1S if he had held five-card support and 4pts) and at least three clubs. This marks him with two or three diamonds. It cannot be right to take a normal finesse, since South knows that West holds Q♦, and there are no weird finesses to be tried, since North-South are missing ♦1098. Therefore, South's only chance is to play for Q♦ to drop. He cashes A♦ and K♦ and, when West does drop Q♦, South's J♦ makes his tenth trick.

Incidentally, for less experienced players, don't lead J♦ from your hand. That is the card with which you are hoping to make your tenth trick. If you lead it, whoever holds Q♦ will put in on top of your J♦ and that will be it. Don't lead a card for a finesse unless you hold the card above or below it also.

See what you make of this auction:

Dealer West

```
              ♠ A92
              ♥ 864
              ♦ A104
              ♣ AQ102
♠ K83                        ♠ J1074
♥ KQ107        N             ♥ J93
♦ 872       W     E          ♦ Q653
♣ K65          S             ♣ 43
              ♠ Q65
              ♥ A52
              ♦ KJ9
              ♣ J987
```

N	E	S	W
–	–	–	NB
1C	NB	2NT	NB
3NT			

North is too strong to open 1NT. In no-trumps, tens are
worth half a point each, making North's hand worth 15pts.
South's 2NT is not my cup of tea, but it showed 10–12pts
and a balanced hand, and North raised to game. West leads
K♥. How should South plan the hand?

Declarer has three or four club tricks, two diamonds, a
heart and a spade. All being well, he will need only one extra trick – perhaps J♦ or Q♠.

Because you must take the club finesse into the East hand, it might be advantageous to hold up A♠ twice, to ensure that East is exhausted, but to assume that West has a five-card suit, and therefore to duck just once, will work fine. Having taken A♥, South leads clubs and takes the successful finesse, ensuring four ticks there. Since there is a two-way finesse in diamonds, that guess should be left until the end, so declarer might try leading a low spade towards his Q♠, and this loses to West's K♠. West cashes any remaining heart winners and, gets off lead, ideally, with another spade. Declarer must now work out who holds Q♦. If he can, the contract will succeed.

Of course, by now, you know who holds Q♦ because you've remembered the auction . . .

West passed originally and has shown up with: ♥KQ, K♠ and K♣. That gives him 11pts and therefore he cannot hold Q♦ or he would have opened the bidding. So, declarer plays a diamond to dummy's A♦ and a low diamond back. When East plays low, he puts on J♦ and makes his ninth trick.

On hands when your opponents have not bid, if one player starts to appear with quite a few points, then he is unlikely to have more than eleven, or he would have bid.

This is why, even when your opponents pass throughout the auction, this is something you must note. The negative inference is that they do not have hands strong enough to open the bidding, or to compete later.

Dealer South ♠ 876
N/S Game   ♥ AQJ
      ♦ AQ10
      ♣ K543

♠ 5   ♠ J10432
♥ 94   ♥ 76532
♦ K9854   ♦ 76
♣ A10976   ♣ 8

      ♠ AKQ9
      ♥ K108
      ♦ J32
      ♣ QJ2

N	E	S	W
–	–	1S	2NT*
Dbl	NB	3NT	NB
6NT			

*Unusual NT Overcall

North-South might have done better to go for a penalty of 3C or 3D but, being vulnerable, South decided to bid the game contract and North, probably somewhat frustrated, raised to the slam.

West's Unusual 2NT overcall is awful. He is under-strength, his suit quality is poor and he is unlikely to buy the contract. However, it will help declarer to plan the play.

West leads 5♦ and South counts his tricks: three spades, three hearts, three diamonds (hopefully) and two clubs. This is one trick short so, unless West mis-defends and rises with his A♣ and takes nothing with it, a fourth spade trick is required.

South runs the lead to his J♦ and leads Q♣ which West wins, before continuing with another low diamond. Declarer takes the finesse which holds and then cashes A♥ and K♥. West follows to both of these tricks. This is interesting since, having shown five clubs and five diamonds, holding two hearts marks West with only one spade – at most. South laid down A♠ and watched West follow to this also. He now felt that West was void in spades so he crossed to dummy with Q♥ and led a spade. When East played low, he put on 9♠ from hand, confident that West was now void. Sure enough, West shows out and the contract is secure.

Your opponents' bidding will assist you when you play the hand, both in terms of point-counts and distribution. It is essential to pay close attention to the bidding, even if your opponents are passing, to make the most of this free information.

In addition, while you are not permitted to take advantage of any information from the look on your partner's face, the speed with which he bids or passes, or the dreadful expressions he pulls whenever you make a bid or lead a card (or is that just *my* partners?), you *can* take advantage of information you glean from your opponents' actions.

At Rubber or Chicago, opponents often think for a while before passing, or consider which lead to make and then come up with something uninspiring. Unless your opponents are known to be slow and dim-witted (I don't know any bridge players who would answer to that description), there is a reason for their uncertainty. Try to read the meaning behind their indecision and you may gain a useful advantage. This is the simple manifestation of what experts call 'Table Presence' – the ability to distil an extra edge from the demeanour of your opponents.

To draw or not to draw – trumps

'Many an old man resides under the arches of Waterloo Bridge because he did not draw trumps soon enough.'

I am sure that an old and wise bridge player has imparted such wisdom to you at some point? Sadly, and like many an old wives' tale, the meaning of such an aphorism is completely misleading. If there are bridge players suffering hardship as a result of their handling of the trump suit, it will almost certainly be because they drew trumps too soon, and not too late.

Having a trump suit is a major advantage, but if you pull all the trumps, the hand often turns into a NT problem and the declarer loses the very advantage for which he has fought in the auction.

Let's start with a very simple example:

Dealer South

	♠ J983	
	♥ 52	
	♦ AQ32	
	♣ A64	

♠ A		♠ 642
♥ QJ1097	N	♥ AK43
♦ 987	W E	♦ 1065
♣ J1083	S	♣ Q97

	♠ KQ1075	
	♥ 86	
	♦ KJ4	
	♣ K52	

N	E	S	W
–	–	1S	NB
3S	NB	**4S**	

West leads Q♥ and South counts four losers: A♠, two hearts and the third round of clubs. However, since dummy has four nice diamonds, declarer can throw away a club loser on the fourth round of diamonds and make the hand. All he must do is avoid an adverse ruff by the opponents.

This is a perfect hand for drawing out the opponents' trumps and I am sure that the vast majority of bridge players would do exactly that.

The point here is that, having drawn trumps, declarer has plenty of tricks with which to fulfil his contract.

Dealer South

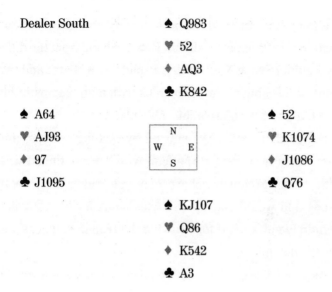

♠ Q983
♥ 52
♦ AQ3
♣ K842

♠ A64
♥ AJ93
♦ 97
♣ J1095

♠ 52
♥ K1074
♦ J1086
♣ Q76

♠ KJ107
♥ Q86
♦ K542
♣ A3

N	E	S	W
–	–	1NT	NB
2C	NB	2S	NB
3S	NB	**4S**	

North-South reach 4S and West leads J♣. In his own hand, declarer can count one spade loser, three heart losers and one possible diamond loser. To draw the trumps here would be a mistake since, without them, South does not have many tricks. To succeed, it appears that the declarer must ruff both a heart and a diamond in dummy. However, this is a poor plan. Instead, as both dummy and his own hand contain four trumps, he should view the hand from the dummy's point of view. Now, he has a spade, two hearts and two clubs to lose, but to ruff two clubs with high trumps in his own hand is a far more achievable plan.

Notice that, had West started by leading trumps, and then, when he regained the lead with A♥, continued with trumps, declarer would have only one trump left in both hands and would end up one trick short for his contract. Definitely not a hand for drawing the trumps – unless you are the defenders.

As you will see in the section on defending, whatever the declarer wants to do, the defence must do the opposite.

When it comes to declarer play, there is nothing I like to do more than to establish a long suit, usually in dummy. To do this, drawing trumps must typically be delayed, since they provide crucial entries into dummy and control of the remaining suits.

Dealer South

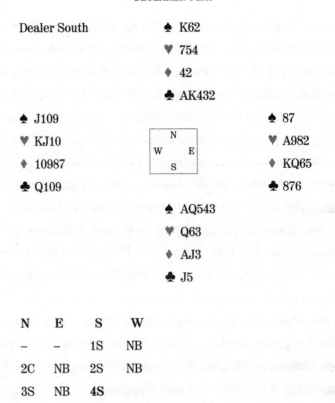

♠ K62
♥ 754
♦ 42
♣ AK432

♠ J109
♥ KJ10
♦ 10987
♣ Q109

N
W   E
S

♠ 87
♥ A982
♦ KQ65
♣ 876

♠ AQ543
♥ Q63
♦ AJ3
♣ J5

N	E	S	W
–	–	1S	NB
2C	NB	2S	NB
3S	NB	**4S**	

North-South squeeze their way into a thin 4S contract and West leads an aggressive J♥. It looks like South has three hearts and two diamonds to lose. One diamond could be trumped in dummy but that won't help if South has already lost four tricks. Dummy's long club suit is declarer's only hope and, outside that suit, there is only one entry to dummy – the trump king.

East overtakes West's lead with A♥ and returns 2♥. West takes both K♥ and 10♥ and switches to 10♦, which South must win. Any temptation to draw trumps must be resisted. Instead, declarer should lead a low club to dummy's A♣, cash K♣ and lead a third club, ruffing it in hand with a low trump. If the club suit does not divide 3-3, the contract is doomed but, today, the bridge gods are on South's side and the clubs do break evenly. Dummy now contains two winning clubs, but they cannot be enjoyed until the trumps are drawn. Added to this, declarer must ensure that he uses dummy's K♠ only at the point when the last trump is extricated from his opponents' hands. South cashes A♠, Q♠ and, sighing with relief that the trump suit has also split kindly, crosses to dummy by playing a third round of trumps to K♠. The trumps are drawn and declarer can pitch both his diamond losers on 4♣ and 3♣. Very satisfying and completely impossible if trumps are drawn too soon.

When you have too many losers in a suit contract, apart from finesses, strange squeezes and mis-defence, there are only two proper ways to develop tricks: trumping in dummy, or establishing a long suit.

When you have too many losers, decide which line you will take before playing the first card from dummy.

Because suit establishment is, in my opinion, the single

most important play technique there is, let's take a look at
a couple more examples:

```
Dealer South              ♠ AQ5
                          ♥ 987
                          ♦ Q8642
                          ♣ 86
        ♠ 832                              ♠ J1097
        ♥ 42            ┌─────────┐        ♥ 653
        ♦ 975          │    N    │        ♦ KJ10
        ♣ AQ1053       │  W   E  │        ♣ K97
                       │    S    │
                       └─────────┘
                          ♠ K64
                          ♥ AKQJ10
                          ♦ A3
                          ♣ J42
```

N	E	S	W
–	–	1H	NB
2H*	NB	**4H**	

* better than 1NT or 2D in response

When the auction consists of only one suit, unless you have
a stand-out lead, a trump is often best (see page 205). West
duly started with 2♥ and it is the best lead. The declarer
has three clubs to lose, plus a diamond. If West had not led

a trump, South would have time to lose a club, then another and still have a trump in dummy to ruff the final club. However, on this defence, he will not have time to do this, since East-West will see the doubleton club in dummy, realize that South wants a ruff, and continue leading trumps.

South's other hope is to establish dummy's diamond suit and he has two spade entries to assist him. He wins trick one and leads A♦ and 3♦, losing to East. East returns a trump, won in South's hand. He crosses to Q♠ and leads a third diamond, ruffing in hand. When the suit divides, his diamonds are good. He draws the last trump, crosses to dummy's A♠ and cashes his diamond winners on which he throws two clubs from hand.

Sometimes, you have to establish a suit whilst keeping an opponent off lead, and with the next deal, remembering the auction will assist you in finding the correct line of play.

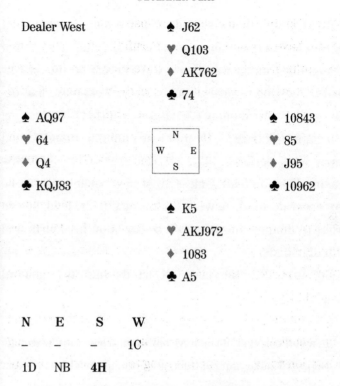

Dealer West

♠ J62
♥ Q103
♦ AK762
♣ 74

♠ AQ97
♥ 64
♦ Q4
♣ KQJ83

N
W E
S

♠ 10843
♥ 85
♦ J95
♣ 10962

♠ K5
♥ AKJ972
♦ 1083
♣ A5

N	E	S	W
–	–	–	1C
1D	NB	**4H**	

South takes a punt at game and West leads K♣. Declarer has two potential spade losers, a diamond and a club. He has a long diamond suit on which he could discard losers but he will have to lose a trick in setting up this suit.

The key to this hand is realizing that if East does not gain the lead, South's K♠ is protected. From the opening bid, West must hold A♠, so if East leads a spade, South's king is dead.

To this end, South should duck the lead, leaving West safely on lead. West may continue with a club or switch to a trump but, either way, South will win and he should now lead a diamond towards dummy. When West plays low, declarer rises with dummy's A♦ and returns to hand, drawing two rounds of trumps. He now leads another diamond and when West, perforce, plays Q♦, declarer must . . . duck – leaving West on lead. Unless West now cashes his A♠, he will never do so, since when South regains the lead, he can cross to dummy and take two discards on his fourth and fifth diamonds.

So, to précis the last few hands into two general principles:

- In a suit contract, if you have sufficient tricks (or few enough losers) to make your contract, draw trumps quickly to prevent your opponents trumping your winning cards.
- If you do not have sufficient tricks to make your contract, there are two main methods to try to create extra tricks: ruffing in dummy or establishing a long suit in dummy. Both these methods usually require delaying drawing trumps until you can see sufficient tricks for your contract. At that point – and remaining aware of entries – draw the opponents' trumps.

Many students confide that they are afraid to delay drawing

trumps in case an opponent trumps in while declarer is trying to make extra tricks. The answer is simple. If you are delaying drawing trumps, it is because you have too few tricks and you are trying to make extra ones. If, while you are trying to do this, something goes wrong, then the contract was probably doomed. At least you have gone down trying to succeed, rather than drawing trumps, playing safe, and committing yourself to failure.

The danger hand

Mainly in no-trump contracts, but sometimes also in suit contracts, there is very often one opponent who poses more of a threat to you than the other. This hand is known as the 'danger hand'. When teaching, I used to place a pair of red devil's horns on the head of the player holding the danger hand, but this practice stopped when a colleague told me she had done this also and, when removing it, found that the student's hair had come with it. The toupee landed in the player's partner's cocktail and, according to my source, the atmosphere of the evening took a marked turn for the worse.

Experienced players have no difficulty identifying the danger hand – it seems easy to them. But, if you have difficulty working out who poses the greater danger, then thinking about it will help.

This is the easy one:

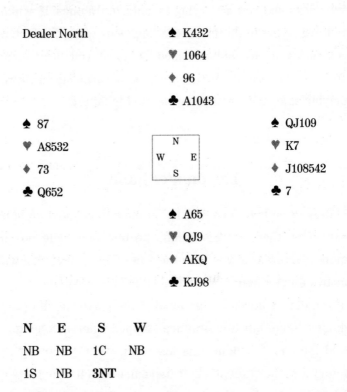

Dealer North

North:
- ♠ K432
- ♥ 1064
- ♦ 96
- ♣ A1043

West:
- ♠ 87
- ♥ A8532
- ♦ 73
- ♣ Q652

East:
- ♠ QJ109
- ♥ K7
- ♦ J108542
- ♣ 7

South:
- ♠ A65
- ♥ QJ9
- ♦ AKQ
- ♣ KJ98

N	E	S	W
NB	NB	1C	NB
1S	NB	**3NT**	

West leads 3♥, which is, presumably, fourth highest. South assumes a five-card suit and counts his tricks. He has two spades, a heart in due course, three diamonds and two clubs. This is eight tricks; one more is required. The club

184

suit is the obvious suit to attack and there is a two-way finesse to take.

East wins with K♥ and returns 7♥. Perhaps West ducks this trick (or perhaps he wins and leads a third heart). Either way, you assume that East no longer holds any hearts. Therefore, he is the safe hand, whereas West, who holds heart winners, is the danger hand. All South must do is play the clubs in such a way as to prevent West from possibly winning a trick.

To do this, make the danger hand play first. Lead 8♣ from hand and, when West plays 2♣, play low from dummy. West cannot win the trick and, even if East could produce Q♣, he would have no hearts left to lead, South would regain control and he has set up his club trick. As it is, East cannot win, so South repeats the finesse through the danger hand, and makes his contract with an overtrick.

Now, try this one:

Dealer South

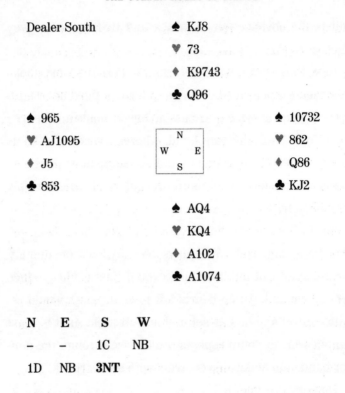

	♠ KJ8	
	♥ 73	
	♦ K9743	
	♣ Q96	

♠ 965		♠ 10732
♥ AJ1095		♥ 862
♦ J5		♦ Q86
♣ 853		♣ KJ2

	♠ AQ4	
	♥ KQ4	
	♦ A102	
	♣ A1074	

N	E	S	W
–	–	1C	NB
1D	NB	**3NT**	

West leads J♥ – top of an internal sequence – and South counts his tricks: three spades, a heart imminently, two diamonds and one club. That is seven tricks. Two more are required. Dummy's diamond suit looks promising, so that will be the suit to attack.

East contributes 2♥ and you decide to win with Q♥. Which opponent is the danger now?

Let's think it through. If we assume that West holds five

hearts, then East started with three. If East had held A♥, he would definitely have played it at trick one because, as far as he knew, East-West could have taken the first five heart tricks. So, East has two low hearts left and West has ♥A10xx. If West gains the lead and plays a heart, your K♥ in your hand is safe. If West leads A♥, your king makes later; if West leads a low heart, your king makes right now. However, if East leads a heart, you will have to decide whether to play your K♥ before West chooses which heart to play – your K♥ will be clobbered sooner or later, and you will lose the next four heart tricks.

So East, with the power to lead through your frail ♥K4, is the danger hand and must be prevented from gaining the lead. When you tackle diamonds, it must done so that East plays first out of your two opponents.

South crosses to dummy with K♠ and leads 3♦. When East plays low, South puts on 10♦ from hand (beating East's card and ensuring that East cannot win the trick). West wins with J♦ but, whatever he leads next, South is in control. When South gains the lead, he cashes A♦, notes that both opponents follow, and then plays 2♦ to K♦, felling East's Q♦ and making the rest of the diamonds.

If this hand seems difficult, I urge you to lay it out – right now – on a table and play through the hand again, reflecting carefully about how you can reproduce these thoughts at the table. Once you master this, it will never be a problem to you again.

I have used this next hand in my classes for many years, and it divides students. It seems impossible to less experienced players, and terribly easy for those with a little more knowledge.

Dealer South

```
                        ♠ 32
                        ♥ A1083
                        ♦ A65
                        ♣ A854
  ♠ AQ8764                              ♠ 109
  ♥ 952             N                   ♥ Q764
  ♦ 84         W         E              ♦ 10972
  ♣ 32             S                    ♣ K96
                        ♠ KJ5
                        ♥ KJ
                        ♦ KQJ3
                        ♣ QJ107
```

N	E	S	W
–	–	1C	1S
3C	NB	**3NT**	

A word or two on the bidding. In the modern style, West might well make a Weak jump-overcall of 2S, but 1S is still just fine. If North-South were playing negative doubles, then North should double. If not, bidding 3C is the next best bid. West leads 7♠; let's plan the play.

South has a spade trick (coming imminently), two hearts, four diamonds and one club. Eight tricks: one more to find. The club suit seems the perfect place, as there are eight cards, missing only the king. Let's see what happens at trick one.

East plays 9♠ and South counts out the suit. He assumes a five-card suit in the West hand, leaving East with three spades. (If West has jump-overcalled to 2S, he will have a six-card suit, leaving East with just two.) To duck this first trick could be disastrous, since East could return a spade and West would take his ♠AQ and all the rest of his spades. So, South wins the first trick with J♠. Since East played 9♠, he might hold 10♠, but he does not hold Q♠ or A♠ as, if he had, he would have played one of those cards. So, West sits with ♠AQxx(x) and East with one or two little spades. Who is dangerous to you?

Again, it is East who poses the threat. If he gains the lead, he can play a spade back through your ♠K5 and West will gobble up all the tricks. This information completely changes South's plan for the hand.

South cannot afford to take the club finesse, since if it loses, East will win the trick. That is too great a risk. Is there a safer alternative?

If, at trick two, South crosses to dummy with A♦, he can then lead 3♥. When East plays low, South puts on J♥. Even if West wins (which, here, he can't), he cannot lead another spade without giving South a trick with his king. Dummy's 10♥ would then be declarer's ninth trick. As it is, J♥ holds the trick and that is South's extra trick straight away. South risked only a finesse into the safe hand and not a finesse into the danger hand.

This is why I say that bridge is a thinking (wo)man's game. You cannot learn this by rote; you have to imagine the consequences of your plays and understand how to pick the safest line of play.

To conclude this little section, here is a hand which features the same problems, but this time with a trump suit.

Dealer South

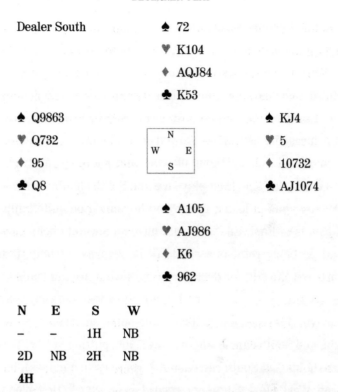

Dealer South ♠ 72
♥ K104
♦ AQJ84
♣ K53

♠ Q9863
♥ Q732
♦ 95
♣ Q8

N
W   E
S

♠ KJ4
♥ 5
♦ 10732
♣ AJ1074

♠ A105
♥ AJ986
♦ K6
♣ 962

N	E	S	W
–	–	1H	NB
2D	NB	2H	NB
4H			

West leads 6♠. What is your plan to secure ten tricks?

The first thing to do is to sigh with relief that West has not led a club. Next, you assess your losers: two in spades, one in hearts, three in clubs. That is a lot of losers. But, there is good news. You have five beautiful diamonds which will provide discards from your hand. In fact, the whole hand comes down to how you tackle the trump suit. There is a two-way finesse against the queen and, unfortunately, you must decide quickly which way to take it. Which opponent presents the most danger to your contract?

West. It is West who can lead a club through dummy's ♣K53 and, if East holds A♣, you will lose three tricks. You don't know that East has A♣; you just assume the worst and see if you can still succeed. East can be allowed on lead, however, since East cannot lead a club without allowing your K♣ to score a trick.

So, at trick one, East plays K♠ and South should . . . duck! Declarer has to lose a spade and he should be quite happy that it is to East. East does not have a pleasant choice now, and probably returns a spade (if he returns a trump, that sorts out the suit for declarer). South wins A♠ and leads J♥ and, when West plays low, dummy plays low too. Only East can win this trick, and he is the safe opponent. East does not win, and South can now lead a low heart, putting in 10♥. This also holds and South can cash K♥, get back to hand with K♦, draw West's last trump and record an overtrick. However, if East had held Q♥, South would still make the hand.

The power of AJ10

If you were offered two suit layouts, such as those below, which would you take?

(a)	**(b)**
♦ AQ3	♦ AJ10
♦ 854	♦ 854

I guess the title of this section gives it away, but you might think that holding ♦AQ would be better than holding ♦AJ. The key factor here is that you also have 10♦ and that makes ♦AJ10 much stronger than ♦AQ3.

If you take the finesse in layout (a), 50 per cent of the time you will score both ace and queen and make two tricks.

If you take two finesses in layout (b), 75 per cent of the time you will score the ace, plus either jack or ten.

This is why AJ10 is so powerful. It is so good, it really should be worth about 7pts, especially in no-trumps. At the very least, think of AJ10 as an ideal opportunity to score two tricks and attack the suit as soon as you can. You lead low towards this holding and, when your left-hand opponent plays low, you put on the ten. You expect this first finesse to lose but, when you regain the lead, play small towards AJ again and, when your left-hand opponent plays low, put on the jack. This time, you expect the finesse to win and, when it does, you have made two tricks.

This deal turned up in a Teams-of-Four match recently.

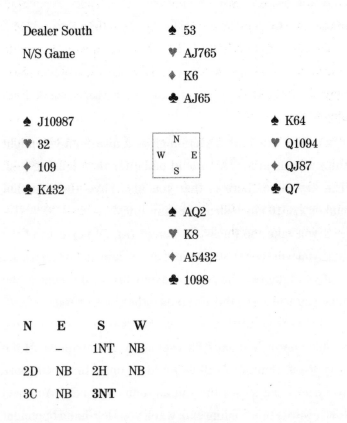

Dealer South

N/S Game

♠ 53
♥ AJ765
♦ K6
♣ AJ65

♠ J10987
♥ 32
♦ 109
♣ K432

N
W   E
S

♠ K64
♥ Q1094
♦ QJ87
♣ Q7

♠ AQ2
♥ K8
♦ A5432
♣ 1098

N	E	S	W
–	–	1NT	NB
2D	NB	2H	NB
3C	NB	**3NT**	

North used a Transfer to show a five-card spade suit, and then showed a four-card club suit. South settled for the NT game. West led J♠. Declarer counted two spade tricks, two hearts, two diamonds and a club. He needs two more tricks. The heart suit might provide these tricks, as might the diamond suit, but both would require considerable luck. The club suit, however, will provide two extra tricks 75 per cent of the time (as long as East does not hold both K♣ and Q♣).

To this end, South ducked trick one and won the spade continuation, before leading 10♣ from hand. When West played small, so did dummy, and East won the trick. East played his last spade, which South won and South then led 9♣. When West played small, dummy also played small and this held the trick. Now, South could play 8♣, West 4♣ and dummy J♣. Three club tricks made his total up to nine and 3NT was made. At the other table, South played on hearts and ended up a trick short.

CHAPTER FOUR

DEFENCE

T HE KEY TO successful defence is to understand how cards work at the bridge table, what the declarer can do to try to make extra tricks and, in direct response to that, what you can do to stop him.

In no-trump contracts, the battle-lines are usually simple: who can establish their long suit first. This is why, generally, once you lead a long suit against a no-trump contract, you should continue with it.

In suit contracts, declarer has two prime methods of making extra tricks: trumping in dummy, and establishing a long suit. If his plan is the former, then to lead trumps will cut down his options; if his plan is the latter, attacking entries to dummy is most likely to stop him from setting up his long suit.

Defending at Duplicate Pairs is often a far more complicated matter. Not only do you have an eye on defeating your opponents' contract, but you must also be aware that you cannot afford to gift him overtricks. This is why judgement in defence at Duplicate is so difficult.

We will return to no-trump contracts later but, to start, let's take a look at defending suit contracts.

Defending trump contracts

When declarer, I am astonished at how often my opponents give me tricks and, in turn, contracts. At bridge clubs throughout the country and especially in private games at home, the defence is, without question, the weakest part of people's games.

When defending suit contracts, for the vast majority of the time, you have only one aim: not to give away tricks to the declarer.

Defending suit contracts can be quite dull, very passive, very disciplined. But those traits will result in declarers failing much more often.

The secret to successful defence is, for the vast majority of the time, the shape of the dummy hand. You can visualize this from the bidding and, of course, see it once it is down on the table.

- If dummy is relatively balanced, your prime objective is not to give away any tricks to the declarer by taking risks in defence.

197

You should lead the safest cards at all times – we'll talk about what those leads are shortly.

- If dummy contains trumps and a shortage in a side-suit, then declarer is likely to want to ruff losers from his hand with dummy's trumps. The way to counter this is to lead trumps, to take them out of dummy before the declarer can use them.

- If there is a long side-suit in dummy, the declarer's plan is probably to establish that side-suit into extra tricks, draw the trumps and then play out his winners. To counter this, you must either take your tricks in the other suits as quickly as possible, or attack the entries into dummy that the declarer may want to use in order to set up his long suit.

This situation – which occurs only rarely – is the one time defenders against a suit contract get to be aggressive and proactive.

FORCING DEFENCE

If the dummy does not contain a long suit – which is most of the time, then this style of defence is certainly what you should be seeking.

The idea is that, since the declarer makes extra tricks only when ruffing in the hand that is short in trumps (usually dummy), to force him to trump in his own hand not only provides a very safe defence, ensuring that you give nothing away, but it also results in the declarer becoming shortened in trumps, sometimes promoting your own modest trump holding into winners.

When you hold four of your opponents' trumps, leading your own long suit, attempting to make the declarer trump in hand, is recommended.

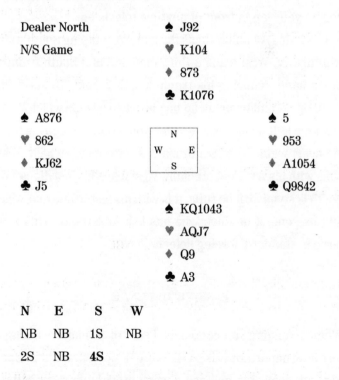

Dealer North		♠	J92
N/S Game		♥	K104
		♦	873
		♣	K1076

♠ A876		♠ 5
♥ 862		♥ 953
♦ KJ62		♦ A1054
♣ J5		♣ Q9842

	♠	KQ1043
	♥	AQJ7
	♦	Q9
	♣	A3

N	E	S	W
NB	NB	1S	NB
2S	NB	**4S**	

Holding four trumps, West should immediately think about

a forcing defence. Clearly, looking at all four hands, you can see that West has only one trump trick. However, if West can reduce South's trump holding, he may promote a second trump trick for himself. West therefore leads his longest suit: 2♦.

Is this a dangerous lead? Yes. But, if you don't want to take risks, just sit at home with your mouth open and the dog on your lap in front of daytime television.

East wins A♦ and returns the suit, West taking South's Q♦ with his K♦. West leads a third diamond and South trumps in his hand, reducing his trump length to four. To succeed, South must pull trumps and he plays two rounds which West must duck. If he stopped now, he would be unable to cash all his heart winners, so South plays a third trump which West wins with his A♠. Now, crucially, West leads his last diamond. South is stymied: if he ruffs, it is with his last trump and West still has one; if he ducks, he has lost four tricks. This is a perfect, standard, forcing defence.

PASSIVE DEFENCE

When defending suit contracts, I cannot emphasize enough just how important it is NOT to break open new suits. Boring, safe, sensible defence always prevails in these situations. Here is a hand from a friendly teams match in which

I played just yesterday at the RAC in Pall Mall, London. I'm
South in 3S.

Dealer West

N/S Game

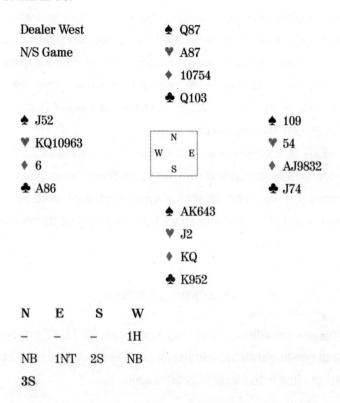

	♠ Q87	
	♥ A87	
	♦ 10754	
	♣ Q103	

♠ J52
♥ KQ10963
♦ 6
♣ A86

♠ 109
♥ 54
♦ AJ9832
♣ J74

♠ AK643
♥ J2
♦ KQ
♣ K952

N	E	S	W
–	–	–	1H
NB	1NT	2S	NB
3S			

West led 6♦ and all seemed reasonably promising; the
contract seems just fine. However, when East wins with A♦
and returns a diamond for West to ruff, things look bleaker.
I have a heart and a club to lose and I will have to guess
who holds J♣. At this stage, I rather favour West to hold it,

since East-West have 16pts between them, West opened the bidding and East has shown up with A♦. Also, since West has only one diamond, he is likely to be longer elsewhere and could have four clubs. All West needs to do now is to play K♥ and the problem is all mine. Instead, at trick three, West kindly switches to 6♣ and my troubles are over: J♣ is located for me, I draw trumps and subsequently just lose the two outstanding aces.

This is a classic example of how the defenders so frequently help the declarer. West should think: dummy is balanced, I have come up with a great lead, all I need to do now is not give anything away. I urge you, when dummy is balanced, think like that.

ATTACKING DEFENCE

On rare occasions – and they really are far less frequent than one might think – dummy's hand is much more threatening. Now is the time to get dynamic.

Dealer East

N/S Game

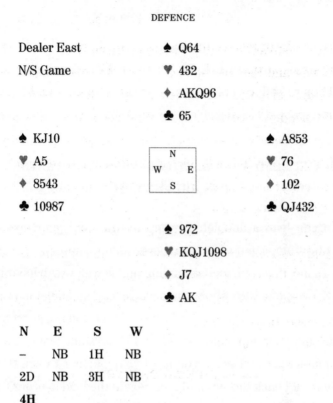

```
             ♠ Q64
             ♥ 432
             ♦ AKQ96
             ♣ 65

♠ KJ10                        ♠ A853
♥ A5            N             ♥ 76
♦ 8543      W      E          ♦ 102
♣ 10987         S             ♣ QJ432

             ♠ 972
             ♥ KQJ1098
             ♦ J7
             ♣ AK
```

N	E	S	W
–	NB	1H	NB
2D	NB	3H	NB
4H			

West makes the safe, passive lead of 10♣ but, as soon as the dummy hits the baize, he should become alert to the imminent danger. Dummy's long diamond suit will provide declarer with at least three, probably five, tricks, and will allow him to discard losers from his hand. This is the moment, in defence, when you must attack – and by that I mean, take your tricks quickly, taking risks to do so – or you will see declarer's losers disappear on the winners in dummy.

When West regains the lead with A♥, he switches to J♠, playing for partner to hold A♠ – this is East-West's only chance. Whether North covers in dummy or not, East-West take their three spade tricks and defeat the contract.

NEVER LEAD A DOUBLETON UNLESS YOUR PARTNER HAS BID THE SUIT

You can lead a doubleton trump to draw out your opponents' trumps, but otherwise, never (almost never).

To me, this is an understanding that is well worth having with everyone with whom you play. To lead a doubleton is a very dangerous and speculative lead. Since you are short in this suit, your opponents are likely to hold some length. For a doubleton to succeed, you need your partner to win the trick, lead back the suit and then regain the lead in order to lead it a third time to give you a ruff.

You will observe a few occasions when leading a doubleton would have made an extra trick. However, you usually do not notice when such a lead gives away a trick or tricks. Leading a doubleton is a hugely losing option in the long run.

An additional benefit to this agreement is that, when you lead a singleton, your partner will not have to wonder whether your lead is a singleton or a doubleton, because he will know it is not a doubleton. Knowing that it is a single-ton will assist your defence immensely.

There is one time when leading a doubleton might be right. When you have a very weak hand and your partner is marked with a strong hand, then it is realistic to assume that he might be strong enough to win your lead, return the suit and, subsequently, regain the lead to provide you with a ruff. However, even in this situation, this is a very attacking, high-risk strategy.

LEADING TRUMPS

Dealer South   ♠ K53

N/S Game   ♥ 76

                     ♦ K632

                     ♣ J865

♠ 872

♥ KJ32

♦ Q1097   N   W   E   S

♣ A2

N	E	S	W
–	–	1S	NB
2S	NB	**4S**	

If you could see the dummy before leading, your conclusion should be that the one asset the dummy contains is his doubleton heart. The declarer may well want to trump hearts in dummy and therefore you should lead trumps as soon as possible to draw them out of the dummy hand.

Against suit contracts, lead a trump if you think that the declarer might want to trump in dummy, or cross-ruff.

Lead a trump if you hold two or three small cards in the trump suit, but do not lead them if you hold a singleton or when you have four of them.

The reason not to lead a singleton trump is that your partner will usually hold three or four trumps and, by leading the suit, you will expose whatever he holds there to an immediate finesse – this is likely to help the declarer more than your side.

When you hold four trumps, you may sacrifice a trick by leading one of them if you have an honour at the head of the suit. In addition, when you have trump length, you want to aim for the aforementioned 'forcing defence' where you lead a long side-suit in the hope of making the declarer trump, reducing his own trump length and making your own even more powerful.

What would you lead from this hand?

Dealer South   ♠ K52

N/S Game   ♥ Q1054

                 ♦ 863

                 ♣ J95

♠ Q943

♥ 8

♦ Q10742   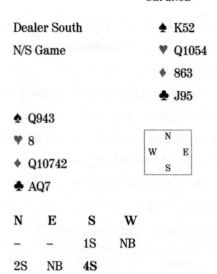

♣ AQ7

N	E	S	W
–	–	1S	NB
2S	NB	4S	

Even seeing the dummy, you might be tempted to lead the wrong suit. The best lead is not your singleton, it is a diamond. This is because, with four trumps, your plan should be to try to force the declarer to trump in his own hand, reducing his trump length and promoting your four trumps into the controlling holding. This way, the declarer loses control. Usually, with four trumps, you lead your longest suit.

If, in this example, South holds five spades, he will be down to four trumps if you can make him trump even once in his hand. This will mean that he cannot draw all your trumps without using all of his. Now where will his tricks come from? The heart suit is breaking badly for him and you are sitting over him with ♣AQ.

If you lead your heart, declarer may well win, draw three trumps and then have time to establish tricks in clubs or hearts.

So, make the declarer trump in his own hand, since this rarely provides him with extra tricks and often shortens his trump holding so that he loses control. Prevent declarer from trumping in dummy (in the hand with the shorter holding in trumps), since those ruffs will provide extra tricks and you want to try to prevent that.

What lead might you consider after this auction?

	West	North	South
♠	942	1C	1S
♥	A643	3C	3S
♦	K872	4S	
♣	Q6		

Let's think about the auction. North has shown a high-quality six-card club suit and probably two-card spade support. South has shown six spades and sufficient points to believe that a game contract is available. What we hold in clubs and spades is very bad news. As we hold three little trumps, even if partner holds a spade honour, it will probably fall under South's top trumps. As we hold the doubleton Q♣, it is likely that the club suit will produce six tricks quickly for declarer whether he plays for the drop or takes the finesse through us.

When dummy contains a long suit, this is the one time to make an aggressive, dangerous lead, in the hope of taking tricks before the declarer draws trumps and plays out his long suit in dummy, throwing away all his losers from his hand.

The lead which offers you the best chance of success is 2♦. Here are the complete hands:

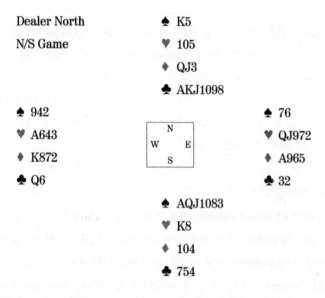

Dealer North	♠ K5
N/S Game	♥ 105
	♦ QJ3
	♣ AKJ1098

West		East
♠ 942		♠ 76
♥ A643		♥ QJ972
♦ K872		♦ A965
♣ Q6		♣ 32

	♠ AQJ1083
	♥ K8
	♦ 104
	♣ 754

Notice that if West leads a trump or a club, South draws trumps, runs his clubs and makes 12 tricks. To lead A♥ or a low card from the heart suit is far too risky, since it allows South to score cards lower than the ace. But, if you lead 2♦,

East will win with A♦ and, seeing dummy's long club suit, will realize that only tricks taken immediately in hearts and diamonds can possibly defeat 4S. East should switch to Q♥. Whatever South does, you make two hearts and two diamonds before he gains the lead.

When dummy contains a long suit, lead an unbid suit and try to take your tricks quickly.

When the dummy contains neither a shortage, nor a long suit (it is balanced), then defence becomes all about not giving away any tricks. If declarer cannot develop extra tricks in the usual ways (trumping in dummy or setting up a long suit) then he has to hope for finesses and defensive errors. So, lead safely at all times.

Safe, passive leads

- These are leads unlikely to give away tricks;
- a trump from two- or three-card holdings of little cards;
- top of a sequence (KQJ, J109) or a broken sequence (KQ10 or J108);
- any suit which the declarer is trumping in his own hand, but not in dummy;
- partner's bid suit.

Aggressive, attacking leads

- A singleton.
- A doubleton (not recommended).
- Low from a suit headed by an honour (K853, Q1042, KJ432).

Use aggressive leads only when dummy contains a long suit, otherwise always make safe leads against suit contracts.

To re-iterate, lead trumps when:

- When your opponents have bid only one suit
- You know, or suspect from the auction, that the declarer is short on points for his contract
- You know, or suspect from the auction, that the dummy is balanced
- Lead a trump, from a two or three-card holding of low cards
- If you know, or suspect from the bidding, that the dummy will contain a long, strong suit, lead an unbid suit with a view to taking your sides' tricks quickly, before declarer can draw trumps and throw his losers away on dummy's long suit.

False-card leads

To false-card, as mentioned earlier, is to play a card that is wrong in your agreed system to confuse the declarer. To be legal, it must also confuse your partner as something that is out of the ordinary. I think that false-carding is dangerous, even for experienced players, but there is one situation in which it is a fine idea.

West

♠ K75

♥ KJ3

♦ 94

♣ AK742

N	E	S	W
–	–	1NT*	NB
3NT			

* 16–18pts

You are on lead and your natural card would be 4♣. You might try A♣, but this is not generally a good idea. Since you hold 14pts, your partner will not hold more than 1pt, so if he misjudges how many cards you hold in clubs, it is unlikely to make any difference since he won't be winning a trick any time soon.

Here, I would lead 2♣. If declarer thinks you have only a four-card club suit, he may play the hand differently from if he suspects you have a five-card suit. He may reject a finesse instead of simply giving up a trick, convinced that you will only have three more club tricks to take. He may reject thoughts of endplaying you, or indeed, seek to endplay you when it is not safe to do so. All being well, when you regain the lead with one of your major suit kings, you will have four club tricks to cash and the contract will be down.

Notice that I have picked a moment where your misinformation will only affect the declarer and not your partner. As a basic guideline I would always suggest leading and discarding honestly because most declarers do not watch these cards as closely as they should and you and your partner are trying to develop an understanding together.

Myths vs science

There are many tales and aphorisms in bridge. Sadly, most of them are unclear and some are just downright wrong. To sort out the myth from the science, here are some of the common ones relating to defence – and the really good tips to have at the back of your mind – and, of course, why.

Never lead away from an ace
As an opening lead against a suit contract, this is true – it is far too dangerous. You may allow an opponent to make a trick with a lower card and, possibly, your ace may be trumped later.

Later in the hand, once you can see dummy and draw some conclusions about who holds what, leading a small card from a suit headed by an ace is just fine.

Leading from an ace against a NT contract is quite acceptable.

Never lead away from a king

It is an aggressive lead, but perfectly acceptable, and a lead you may well have to make. To lead top of a sequence is safe and attacking but you do not always have the luxury of holding sequences.

Lead through strength

Not a bad tip, but incomplete and, as such, dangerous. By all means lead through a short, strong holding towards your partner's hand, but never lead dummy's (or the declarer's) long suit, since this is probably exactly what the declarer would like to do.

Incidentally, the player sitting to the declarer's right always has an easier time defending than his partner. This is because a very good principle is always to attack the suit that is weak to your right. Dummy is to this player's right and he can see which suit offers potential. Conversely, the leader has the declarer on his right, and cannot see that hand. He must remember the bidding, interpret the declarer's play and watch for partner's signals to help decide what to do.

In defence, do NOT lead dummy's long suit.

Always lead the top card in your partner's suit
Rarely lead the top card in your partner's suit! This is an awful one because it prevents your partner from distinguishing what you might hold in his suit. As a general rule, when leading partner's bid suit:

- Lead top of any touching honour cards, down to 109, regardless of how many cards you hold in his suit.
- Lead the higher of two cards.
- Lead MUD (middle-up-down) or top-of-rubbish with three or four low cards.
- Lead low when you have an honour or broken honours at the head of a three- or four-card suit.

Never let the declarer trump
This is nonsense. Try to stop the dummy from trumping, but if by leading a suit you make the declarer trump in his own hand, this is safe for you and, quite possibly, attacking also, since declarer will use the trump length in his hand and end up with fewer trumps with which to draw yours. This is known as a forcing defence (see page 198).

215

Always lead an ace against a slam

Poppycock! At Duplicate Pairs, there might be a good reason to lead an unsupported ace (an ace without the king beneath it) to prevent an overtrick, but at Rubber Bridge, Chicago and Teams-of-Four your aim is to defeat the contract. More slams have been given away by an opponent leading an ace without holding the king than have ever been defeated by leading that ace. Aces are meant for taking kings and queens; if you lead one, everyone plays low cards.

When you have AK in a suit, always lead them

No – please, no. When you have AK at the head of the suit, you lead the ace, and you watch your partner's signal very carefully. Most people will play that a high card encourages you to play your king and a low card asks you not to play your king. If you play your king without thought, you will simply promote your opponents' queen into a trick. That is terrible play.

It's automatic; you don't even need to think

It's never automatic and it's always right to think. I would far rather take a few seconds longer and make the right decision than hurry and make the wrong one.

You do not always return your partner's lead; you do not always play low second-in-hand and high third-in-hand (although these are decent basic generalizations). Each hand requires consideration and thought.

And here are a few key principles on opening and later leads which, if you adopt these within your partnership, will improve your defence immediately:

- The three key leads: (1) honour card promises top of a sequence, or top of a broken sequence; (2) low card promises a suit headed by an honour or broken honours; (3) high intermediate card suggests top-of-rubbish.
- If the declarer is not drawing trumps, draw them for him.
- If there is a shortage in dummy, lead trumps.
- Never lead a doubleton – unless it is your partner's bid suit.
- Never lead dummy's long suit.
- When your opponents have bid only one suit, unless you have a very safe lead, try playing a trump.

Interpreting the auction

Since opening leads are made blind, the bidding is your only guide. Based on some of the key principles discussed above, let's look at some auctions and decide what to lead.

	(a)		**(b)**	
West	**N**	**S**	**N**	**S**
♠ 732	1D	1S	1D	1S
♥ KJ53	2S	3S	3D	3S
♦ 84			**4S**	
♣ AQ63				

(a) North-South have meandered into 4S without much conviction, and they are probably lacking high-card points. When this is the case, they may be hoping to make up for having few points by trumping. For this reason, leading a trump is usually best; say 2♠.

(b) North has six good diamonds; South six spades. You need to take what tricks you have quickly, before declarer draws trumps and pitches his losers from hand on dummy's diamonds. Make an attacking lead of 3♥.

	(c)	
West	**N**	**S**
♠ Q32	1D	1S
♥ KJ53	1NT	3S
♦ Q4	4S	
♣ 10983		

(c) North has rebid 1NT, strongly suggesting a balanced hand in dummy. When the dummy is balanced, your aim is always to lead as safely as possible. Each suit carries some risk, but your modest sequence in clubs seems best. 10♣ should be your opening lead.

(d)

West	N	E	S	W
♠ 8632	–	1S	2D	3S
♥ AQJ	4D	4S	NB	NB
♦ A32	5D	NB	NB	**Dbl**
♣ 973				

(d) When your opponents sacrifice against your game contract, they will be doing so based, not on points, but mostly on trump length. As ever, when your opponents are short of points, they will be seeking ruffs. That is why, very often, against a sacrifice contract, your best lead will be a trump to cut down the number of ruffs your opponents can make. On this hand, where I expect my partner to hold only one trump, I would lead A♦ and another to get two rounds of trumps out immediately.

Whenever you think your opponents are short of points for their contract and/or will want to use trumps for ruffing (opposed to drawing the trumps), then lead trumps yourself - and keep leading them.

Defending NT contracts

Defending NT contracts has a certain simplicity about it. The declarer is counting tricks and deciding from where he is going to find the extra tricks; you should be trying to establish your side's longest suit to take more tricks than the declarer can afford to lose. As a basic background thought, it is usually right to continue to play the suit led, as opposed to switching from one suit to another.

There are some key principles which will simplify your life, and perhaps the most important of these is to lead the right card from the right suit.

OPENING LEADS AGAINST NT CONTRACTS

In no-trumps, the declarer has the advantage of being able to see both his partnership's hands; the defenders have the advantage of making the opening lead. The side that gets their suit established first will often prevail, so the defenders' advantage here is substantial.

The traditional 'fourth highest of your longest and strongest' is fair enough, but it ignores many additional opportunities.

When you pick a suit to lead, generally it will be one unbid by your opponents, of decent quality and from a hand that contains entries (means of regaining the lead later). The longest of these suits is usually best. Indeed, four-card suits are not desirable leads; a five-card suit is much more likely to be successful.

Let's take a look below at the various types of standard lead available:

SEQUENCES

(a) **AKQ**54   **KQJ**64   **QJ**105   **J**10932   **10**983

Top of a sequence is a lead of ace, king, queen, jack or ten, which promises the two cards beneath the one led. This is the best lead because it is both safe (you won't give anything away) and also attacking (because you are pushing out your opponents' high cards and trying to establish your low cards into winners.

If you have 987, that is not a sequence; a sequence must contain at least one honour card.

(b) **KQ**105   **QJ**942   **J**10843

These are top of broken sequence leads: two cards touching one another at the head of the suit and then the next but one card in sequence. This is also a very good lead.

(c) A**J**1083   K**J**1083   Q**10**983

These are internal sequence leads. You still promise the card beneath the one you have led, but you may have a card higher than your lead (but it will not be touching the card you led).

If you have no type of sequence, then fourth highest from a suit headed by an honour or broken honours is advised.

(d)   AJ742   KJ83   K9632

This lead of a low card suggests interest in the suit, and asks your partner to try to win the trick and return your suit, either immediately or, if partner can only win a trick later, then subsequently in the hand.

(e)   9753   107432   8753

When you have no honour in the suit, but you feel that the suit will be the safest lead available, lead top-of-rubbish. If your suit is headed by the ten, you might want to lead second highest to preserve your ten for later.

The key here is that your partner must interpret your lead before playing to the first trick:

- Honour = top of sequence, broken sequence or internal sequence.
- Low card = fourth highest from a suit headed by an honour or broken honours.
- High intermediate card = from a useless suit containing no honours.

THE DUTY OF THE LEADER'S PARTNER

When defending no-trump contracts, the spotlight really is on you. Your basic duty is to cooperate with your partner's lead and, unless you are certain there is a good alternative, regain the lead quickly and return partner's suit.

If your partner leads top-of-rubbish, you may choose whether to try to win the trick or not, and you do not need to return the suit unless you believe it is your only hope of beating the contract.

If your partner leads a low card, suggesting a fourth-highest lead, your duty is to try to win the trick and return the suit to your partner, either immediately or, if you cannot win the first trick, as soon as you do regain the lead.

If your partner leads an honour card, suggesting a lead from one of the various sequences, your duty is to play any honour card you have immediately, even if this means over-taking your partner's card with a higher one, or jettisoning a lower honour card. This will inform partner as to where the missing honour cards are located and unblock the suit to ensure that you are playing the high card from the short-er holding – almost always a good idea when playing out a long suit, both as defenders and as the declarer.

This last duty – jettisoning and overtaking – is quite counter-intuitive, but let's see why you should do it.

Dealer South

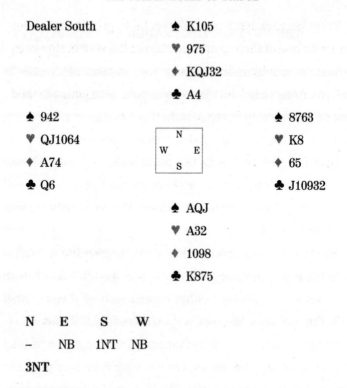

```
                        ♠ K105
                        ♥ 975
                        ♦ KQJ32
                        ♣ A4
♠ 942                                        ♠ 8763
♥ QJ1064          N                          ♥ K8
♦ A74          W     E                       ♦ 65
♣ Q6              S                          ♣ J10932
                        ♠ AQJ
                        ♥ A32
                        ♦ 1098
                        ♣ K875
```

N	E	S	W
–	NB	1NT	NB
3NT			

West leads Q♥; East plays low and South ducks. West plays another heart, East plays K♥ and South ducks. That is the end of the defence. East cannot lead any more hearts and the declarer will make his contract easily.

If East plays K♥ on top of West's Q♥ and leads back his 8♥, West can continue playing hearts until South wins and, when West regains the lead with A♦ – which he will – he can take sufficient heart winners to defeat the contract. Simple.

Many players hate to overtake their partner's honour card with one of their own, considering it a waste. However, to block a suit by failing to play your honour at the start will lead to more of your opponents' contracts making – and that will prove very costly.

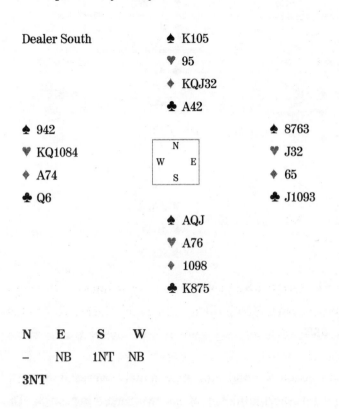

Dealer South

♠ K105
♥ 95
♦ KQJ32
♣ A42

♠ 942
♥ KQ1084
♦ A74
♣ Q6

♠ 8763
♥ J32
♦ 65
♣ J1093

♠ AQJ
♥ A76
♦ 1098
♣ K875

N	E	S	W
–	NB	1NT	NB
3NT			

West leads K♥ and East drops J♥. He does this to tell West that South does not hold J♥ and it is safe for West to continue leading hearts from the top until A♥ is dislodged. East can be quite confident that this is safe since West must be promising KQ10. If East does not drop J♥, he denies that he holds it.

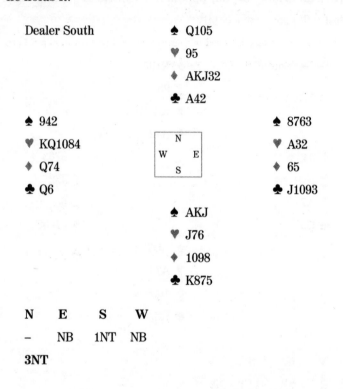

Dealer South

North: ♠ Q105 ♥ 95 ♦ AKJ32 ♣ A42

West: ♠ 942 ♥ KQ1084 ♦ Q74 ♣ Q6

East: ♠ 8763 ♥ A32 ♦ 65 ♣ J1093

South: ♠ AKJ ♥ J76 ♦ 1098 ♣ K875

N	E	S	W
–	NB	1NT	NB
3NT			

West leads K♥ and East immediately overtakes with A♥ and returns the higher of his two remaining cards. This way, East-West take the first five tricks. If East does not play A♥, he denies holding it.

The only, very rare, occasions when you do not immediately overtake or jettison an honour are when:

(a) you believe you have more cards in the suit than your partner – perhaps when you hold five of them;

(b) when you can see a card in dummy which you will definitely promote if you do overtake. See below:

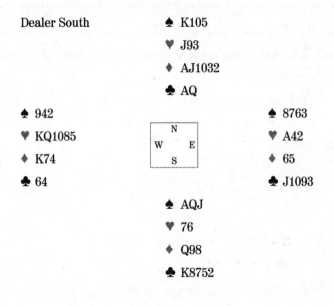

Dealer South

♠ K105
♥ J93
♦ AJ1032
♣ AQ

♠ 942
♥ KQ1085
♦ K74
♣ 64

♠ 8763
♥ A42
♦ 65
♣ J1093

♠ AQJ
♥ 76
♦ Q98
♣ K8752

N	E	S	W
–	NB	1NT	NB
3NT			

West leads K♥ and East immediately knows that his partner holds a suit headed by ♥KQ10. If East overtakes K♥ with A♥ here, he can see that this will promote dummy's J♥ into a trick. Therefore, on this occasion, he does not overtake. West should be able to work out that East has A♥ because, if South held it, he would surely win the first trick, knowing that J♥ in dummy was a second stopper. When East does not win the first trick, West should think this through and then lead a low heart to East's A♥; a heart will then come back so that West can cash his three further winners.

Remembering the duty of leader's partner, take a look at this hand – a classic I set to all my more advanced students:

Dealer South

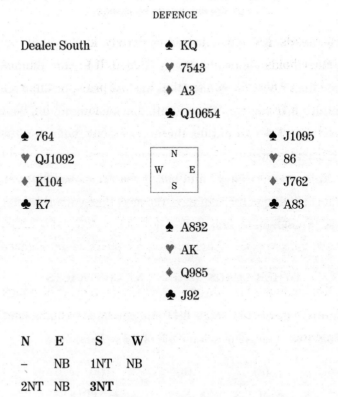

♠ KQ
♥ 7543
♦ A3
♣ Q10654

♠ 764　　　　　　　　　♠ J1095
♥ QJ1092　　　　　　　♥ 86
♦ K104　　　　　　　　♦ J762
♣ K7　　　　　　　　　♣ A83

♠ A832
♥ AK
♦ Q985
♣ J92

N	E	S	W
–	NB	1NT	NB
2NT	NB	**3NT**	

West leads Q♥, dummy and East play low and South wins with K♥. Declarer plays a spade to dummy's K♠ and leads 4♣. East plays low and West wins before leading J♥. South wins this and plays another club, which East wins with A♣. However, East now has no heart to lead and the declarer will make his contract.

East forgot his duty. As leader's partner, he must try to win a trick as quickly as possible and, unless he is certain it is the wrong thing to do, return partner's led suit.

Watch what happens. Declarer leads 4♣ from dummy, East hops up with A♣ and leads his last heart, pushing out South's last stopper. When South plays another club, West wins with K♣ and cashes three more heart winners. The contract is down.

This is not an easy hand but, if you remember the principle behind good NT defence, the next time you are sitting East, you might be able to find it.

OTHER LEADS AGAINST NT CONTRACTS

Your opponents bid 1NT – 3NT and you have to find a lead. What would you choose on each of these hands?

	(a)	(b)	(c)
♠	AQ1085	J842	743
♥	632	K42	J8
♦	J65	Q2	8732
♣	86	A964	5432

(a) AQ10 is a very difficult holding from which to lead. However, to lead a fourth-highest card is too risky as it may allow a very low card to win the first trick. With no outside entry to your hand – as you have here – you would usually lead the queen, allowing you to look at dummy, your partner's card and what the declarer does. At worst, this will lose to the king and your suit headed by A10 may still prove a considerable threat.

If you do have an outside entry – perhaps an ace in an outside suit – you can lead the ace, look at dummy, partner's card and what the declarer does, and then decide whether to continue leading your suit and, if so, with which card. So, from this hand – without the outside entry – lead Q♠. This isn't perfect, but it is a major improvement over leading fourth highest.

(b) The worst lead against a no-trump contract is, without doubt, a four-card suit headed by the jack (if you have J109x, then to lead the jack is fine). Avoid leading fourth highest from such a suit; it nearly always gives away a trick and is rarely a good enough suit ever to be established profitably. Lead 4♣ instead.

(c) When you have a very weak hand, you must think differently. Your strategy is to lead your side's longest and best suit, regain the lead and continue leading it until your low cards are promoted into winners. When you have a very weak hand, you must try to lead your partner's longest suit. Here, I would try J♥ (you can lead a doubleton against a no-trump contract – very rarely). If your partner has a five-card heart suit, you will be a hero. If not, you won't be, but I, for one, am used to that.

Signals and discards

When you play with a new partner, discuss your bidding system. But, always leave time to talk about defence as well. These are the main topics, discussed more below:

WHAT SIGNALS DO YOU PLAY?

Usually, you will play Attitude Signals (I like your lead, or I don't like it) and/or Count Signals (how many cards you hold in the suit).

WHAT DO YOUR DISCARDS MEAN?

I play that I always throw away from the suit I am least interested in my partner leading, usually my weakest suit. Within that discard, I might apply a Suit-preference Discard (sometimes called a 'McKenney Discard').

DO YOU PLAY SUIT-PREFERENCE LEADS?

Automatically, you should: when you are leading a card for your partner to trump; when you are clearing a suit in a NT contract.

ATTITUDE SIGNALS

A very simple principle: when your partner leads an ace, or
if he leads a low card and dummy plays the ace, play a high
card if you like your partner's lead; a low card if you do not
like partner's lead.

Dealer South   ♠ 864

N/S Game   ♥ K943

      ♦ AKJ4

      ♣ J7

A ♠ led

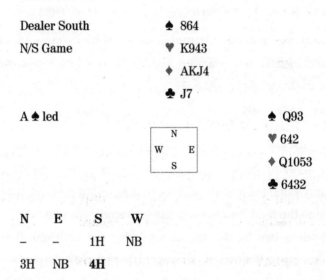

      ♠ Q93

      ♥ 642

      ♦ Q1053

      ♣ 6432

N	E	S	W
–	–	1H	NB
3H	NB	**4H**	

Your partner leads A♠, promising the king, he wants to
know if you can win the third round. If you can, he wants
you to encourage; if not, to discourage. You will win the
third round if you hold the queen or a doubleton, when you
can trump the third round. So, here, you play 9♠.

Dealer South   ♠ A63

N/S Game   ♥ K943

                 ♦ AKJ4

                 ♣ J7

                                  ♠ K84

4♠ led
             N   ♥ 642

          W   E

             S   ♦ Q1053

                                  ♣ 6432

N	E	S	W
–	–	1H	NB
3H	NB	**4H**	

Your partner leads 4♠, suggesting three or four cards to an honour or broken honours. If declarer plays A♠ from dummy, encourage your partner to play another spade if he regains the lead, by an encouraging signal. Play 8♠.

Holding two cards, you always play the high one first to indicate a doubleton. However, there is one important exception. When you have the queen, you only play it if it is your only card, or if you also hold the jack. Knowing this, partner could under-lead his king, allowing you to win the next trick and have you on lead.

For this reason, if partner leads an ace and you hold queen-small, you do not play the queen, but the low card instead.

These are the two occasions I would play an Attitude Signal: when partner leads an ace; when partner leads a card and the opponent next to play rises with the ace. Please note that an Attitude Signal is only made when your partner has led. A little phrase to help you: 'ace asks for attitude'.

At all other times, including those when your opponent leads the suit, and you are not involved in trying to win the trick, you should choose to show your count (how many cards you hold in the suit).

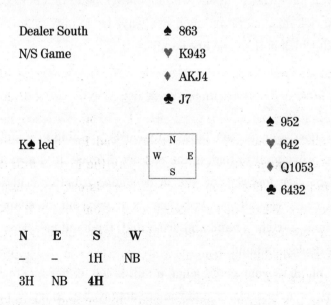

Dealer South	♠ 863
N/S Game	♥ K943
	♦ AKJ4
	♣ J7

♠ 952
♥ 642
♦ Q1053
♣ 6432

K♠ led

N	E	S	W
–	–	1H	NB
3H	NB	**4H**	

Partner leads K♠ and you drop 2♠, indicating that you hold an odd number of cards in the suit. Partner will usually assume that you have three and he can count out the suit and work out how many spades the declarer holds.

You would use the same idea in no-trump contracts also.

NB: Most people play these signals as above but there is a growing opinion that to play the signals in a reverse fashion is better. That would mean for Attitude Signals a high card is discouraging, a low card encouraging, and for Count Signals, a high card indicates an odd number; a low card an even number. I confess, I like this method. However, if you play with someone who has never done this before, you risk misunderstandings, so always try to play systems with which both of you are happy.

COUNT SIGNALS

To show your partner how many cards you hold in a suit can prove vital to finding the correct defence. It is also a major step forward for you in becoming a better bridge player as all really good players try to work out the shape of their partner's hand and, from that, the hand pattern of the declarer's hand.

You show your count when a suit is led, either by your partner or by declarer, and you are not involved in trying to win the trick.

Note that you will *not* show count if your partner has

led an ace, or your partner leads a card and the first opponent to play rises with the ace. In those situations, you show your attitude (as described in the previous section).

Additionally, against no-trump contracts, you will *not* show count if your partner has led an honour card and you hold an honour card with which you can overtake the trick, or jettison a lower honour card.

The standard method of showing count is to play a low card to indicate an odd number of cards held in the suit (this is very often three), and a high card to indicate an even number of cards held in the suit (this is nearly always two or four – and the bidding will guide you as to which is the more likely).

There is an alternative method called 'Reverse Count' which can, sometimes, have some advantages. This involves doing the opposite to above. However, the vast majority of the world play the standard method.

It is good to get into the habit of showing count even if your partner is not paying much attention (the assumed state of most partners, I fear) since, when you do play with someone who watches every card you play, you will then be able to inform them accurately about the shape of your hand.

Let's take a look at a couple of examples to show you how useful showing count – and interpreting it – can be:

Dealer South

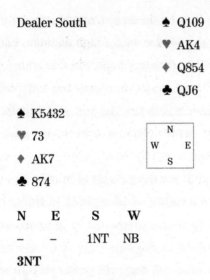

♠ Q109
♥ AK4
♦ Q854
♣ QJ6

♠ K5432
♥ 73
♦ AK7
♣ 874

N	E	S	W
–	–	1NT	NB
3NT			

South opens a Weak NT and is raised to 3NT. As West, you lead your fourth highest spade – 3♠ – and declarer plays 9♠ from dummy, your partner 6♠, and declarer wins with J♠. South now leads a diamond from hand. What do you know, and what should you do?

Here, the count is vital. Your partner has played his lowest spade on the first trick, indicating an odd number of cards in the spade suit – probably three. If he holds only one card, then it looks unlikely you can defeat the contract but, if he holds three, that means the declarer started with only two cards in spades. Since you know that your partner does not hold A♠ – as he would have won the first trick and returned the lead to you – declarer must hold A♠ and have started with ♠AJ doubleton. Since it appears that he needs a diamond trick(s) to make his contract, you should rise with a high diamond and play another low spade. The declarer must win this with A♠ and, when you get the chance to win your other top diamond, you lead K♠ to smother dummy's Q♠ and you will take the remaining three spade tricks to defeat the contract.

Note that, when thinking about the count, always consider how many cards each hand held in each suit originally. If you try to think about what each player has left after each trick, you will make yourself dizzy. Always think about the original hand pattern.

Take a look at this next hand and see if you can assess the exact shape of the declarer's hand?

Dealer South

		♠ AK43	
		♥ K76	
		♦ Q8	
		♣ 8543	
♠ Q652			
♥ 54		N	
♦ A7	W		E
♣ KQJ96		S	

N	E	S	W
–	–	1H	NB
1S	NB	2D	NB
4H			

239

You sensibly decide to lead K♣ against South's 4H contract and notice that your partner plays 10♣, before the trick is taken by South's A♣. Your partner's high card suggests an even number of cards held in clubs. While it could be a singleton, if it was, this would make it likely that South held three spades and, with that holding, he might well have supported his partner rather than rebidding 2D. So, it looks like partner has two clubs, leaving declarer with two clubs. Remembering the auction, West can now assume that South holds five hearts and four diamonds, probably two clubs and therefore probably two spades, making his original shape (or 'hand pattern' as experts like to call it): 2-5-4-2.

On this hand, knowing the declarer's shape may not help much, other than to remind you not to discard a spade, but merely having a 95 per cent certain idea of the declarer's shape at trick one can prove incredibly useful and, indeed, crucial to improving your defence.

Most importantly, when you make Count or Attitude Signals, please make them clear.

- When you play a low card – play your lowest.
- When you play a high card - play the highest possible card you can afford.

SUIT-PREFERENCE LEADS

If I sat down in a bridge club, I probably wouldn't discuss these because I would expect them to be played automatically. I would expect, but I might be disappointed.

There are two main occasions when you would use this lead:

Dealer South	♠ Q52
N/S Game	♥ A1054
	♦ K2
	♣ Q965

♠ AK1063
♥ 82
♦ A43
♣ 732

```
    N
W       E
    S
```

N	E	S	W
–	–	1H	1S
3H	NB	**4H**	

As West, you lead A♠ and watch carefully for your partner's Attitude Signal. He plays J♠. This looks encouraging and as if he holds a doubleton, so you lead K♠ and he plays 7♠. You are now going to lead a third spade for him to trump.

The size of the card you lead now indicates which suit you would like led back once he has ruffed. Being trumps, hearts are out of the picture. If you wanted a club led – the lower-ranking suit – you would lead your lowest spade, the three; if, as you do here, you want a diamond – the higher-ranking suit – led back, you lead your highest spade, 10♠.

The other occasion occurs in no-trumps, when you are clearing a long suit:

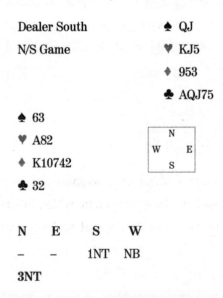

Dealer South   ♠ QJ

N/S Game   ♥ KJ5

      ♦ 953

      ♣ AQJ75

♠ 63

♥ A82

♦ K10742

♣ 32

N	E	S	W
–	–	1NT	NB
3NT			

West leads 4♦ against South's 3NT contract. East wins with A♦ and returns 8♦ on which South plays J♦. South definitely has Q♦ (because if East had held it, he would have

242

played it back to you), so West wins and prepares to lead a third diamond to knock out South's final stopper. At this stage, the size of the card West leads will indicate to East in which suit West holds an entry. Clubs are clearly out of the picture, so the choice is between hearts and spades. Since West wants a heart returned, the lower-ranking suit, he leads his 2♦.

Once you know to look for these signals they are super-powerful and easy to follow. If you and your partner/group don't make these signals, it is well worth sitting down to chat about them, practising and becoming familiar with them.

THE KEY TO SIGNALS

This section is not about the signals themselves, but how you interpret them. This is a classic problem, which incorporates many of the elements of defence at which we've been looking.

Dealer North

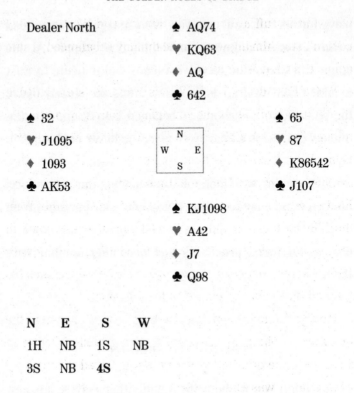

♠ AQ74
♥ KQ63
♦ AQ
♣ 642

♠ 32   ♠ 65
♥ J1095   ♥ 87
♦ 1093   ♦ K86542
♣ AK53   ♣ J107

♠ KJ1098
♥ A42
♦ J7
♣ Q98

N	E	S	W
1H	NB	1S	NB
3S	NB	**4S**	

West leads A♣ and East drops 7♣. Taking this as encouraging, West leads K♣ and, then, 5♣. South wins his Q♣, loses K♦ later, and makes his contract.

Well, this is about as bad as it gets, but it is typical of standard defence. Let's think a little more about this hand.

West has come up with the correct lead. Dummy comes down without a long threatening suit and without much of a shortage. As dummy holds ♦AQ, it is unlikely that declarer will want to ruff a diamond in dummy and West probably couldn't stop him anyway. So the dummy is balanced; a safe defence is what is required.

When East drops 7♣ on West's A♣, this is an Attitude Signal, encouraging or discouraging a continuation in diamonds. But, is 7♣ high or low? The key will lie in its relative value. West looks at his hand and at dummy. He notes that 2♣, 3♣, 4♣, 5♣ and 6♣ are in those two hands. Therefore, East's 7♣ is low, asking him not to lead another club. West dutifully switches to 10♦, leading through short strength in dummy. Whether East is allowed to win this trick now or later, when he does, he returns J♣, South never makes his Q♣ and the declarer goes off in his 4S game.

Passive defence, giving nothing away, defeats the contract. Looking at the size of your partner's card in relation to the others that are showing solved the mystery of whether it was high or low.

If your partner plays a 4, and you cannot see either the 2 or 3 in your hand, dummy, or played by the declarer, the 4 is likely to be high. Conversely, an 8 may be low – you just have to take time to work it out. Even then, it may be impossible to tell, but at least you've tried to play the game.

The size of the card your partner plays can only be interpreted by looking at all the other cards available in that suit.

CHAPTER FIVE

ENJOY YOUR BRIDGE

So, THAT'S IT. You have looked at many of the key bids, plays and defensive understandings. If my partner did all of these relatively simple things well, I would have a great game with him or her. Winning at bridge, be it Duplicate or Rubber Bridge, is about making as few mistakes as possible, thinking about what is going on at all times, concentrating.

I once took a private class of ladies during the Wimbledon Tennis Championships. The television was on – with the volume off – a large dog was stalking the tea trolley and pushing its nose into students' laps, and there was a bowl of pistachio nuts which were proving quite a struggle to free from their shells. With all this going on, bridge came a poor fourth and, as a result, the standard was appalling. Some background noise is pretty typical, but generally, focus. You will enjoy the game so much more.

And one more thing: please don't lecture your partner at

the table. A quiet word afterwards is fine. Lecturing them destroys your partner's confidence, embarrasses the opposition and makes you look like a complete nitwit. Man management is at an all-time low and the bridge room is no exception. Don't think that being loyal to your partner is somehow a sign of weakness. The best partners are utterly loyal and then, later, in private, they may provide a short (or, in my case, long) lecture. That's a much better way to behave.

Good luck.